Low Fat Chicken

Low Fat Chicken

LORENZ BOOKS

NEW YORK • LONDON • SYDNEY • BATH

This edition published in 1997 by Lorenz Books

This edition published in the USA by Lorenz Books
27 West 20th Street, New York, NY 10011

LORENZ BOOKS are available for bulk purchase for sales promotion and for
premium use. For details write or call the manager of special sales: Lorenz Books,
27 West 20th Street, New York, NY 10011; (800) 354 9657

ISBN 1 85967 472 0

Publisher: Joanna Lorenz
Senior Cookery Editor: Linda Fraser
Project Editor: Anne Hildyard
Assistant Editor: Margaret Malone
Designer: Alan Marshall
Photographers: Karl Adamson, Edward Allwright, David Armstrong, James Duncan,
Michelle Garrett, Amanda Heywood, David Jordan and Peter Reilly
Recipes: Catherine Atkinson, Christine France, Shirley Gill, Shehzad Husain,
Sue Maggs, Liz Trigg and Steven Wheeler
Food for photography: Nicola Fowler, Jane Stevenson, Judy Williams
and Elizabeth Wolf-Cohen
Stylists: Madeleine Brehaut, Hilary Guy, Jo Harris and Blake Minton

Printed and bound in Hong Kong

1 3 5 7 9 10 8 6 4 2

Some of the recipes have previously been published as part of other Anness titles.

CONTENTS

INTRODUCTION

Chicken is a popular food and rightly so. It is economical, quick to prepare and it is endlessly versatile, adapting to any cooking method. Chicken can be poached, stir-fried, roasted, crumbed and baked, casseroled and sautéed and combines well with just about any ingredient or flavor.

Although chicken has less fat and fewer calories than red meat, it is low in fat only when the skin is removed. Removing the skin lowers the fat by as much as 50 percent. Fortunately, cooking chicken with the skin, which adds flavor and retains moisture, then removing the skin before serving, will still give the reduced fat benefits.

Some of the recipes in *Low Fat Chicken* have been cooked in their skin for flavor retention or because the design of the recipe dictates that this is the best method. In these recipes, strip off the skin after cooking or before eating to minimize fat intake.

Cutting down on fat doesn't have to mean losing out on flavor, and there is no need to forgo your favorite chicken dishes, as the recipes in this book show. *Low Fat Chicken* will help you make healthier choices of cooking methods that will ensure you enjoy chicken as much as ever.

Facts about Fats

It's important to know something about different fats before we can make changes to the way we eat – some fats are believed to be less harmful than others.

Fats in our foods are made up of building blocks of fatty acids and glycerol and their properties vary according to each combination. There are three main types of fatty acids; saturated, polyunsaturated and unsaturated or mono-unsaturated. There is always a combination of each of the three types in any food, but the amount of each type varies greatly from one food to another.

SATURATED FATS

All fatty acids are made up of chains of carbon atoms. Each atom has one or more free 'bonds' to link with other atoms and by doing so the fatty acid transports nutrients to cells throughout the body. Without these free 'bonds' the atom cannot form any links, that is to say, it's completely 'saturated'. Because of this, the body finds it hard to process the fatty acid into energy, so simply stores it as fat.

The main type of saturated fat is found in food of animal origin – meat and dairy products such as lard and butter, which are solid at room temperature. However, there are also some saturated fats of vegetable origin, notably coconut and palm oils. A few margarines and oils are processed by changing some of the unsaturated fatty acids to saturated ones; these are labelled 'hydrogenated vegetable oil' and should be avoided.

MONOUNSATURATED FATS

These are found in foods such as olive oil, rapeseed oil (canola), some nuts, oily fish and avocados. They may help lower the blood cholesterol and this could explain why in Mediterranean countries there is such a low incidence of heart disease.

Above: *Some oils such as olive and rapeseed (canola) are thought to help lower blood cholesterol.*

Above left: *Animal products such as lard and butter and some margarines are major sources of saturated fats.*

Right: *Vegetable and plant oils and some margarines are high in polyunsaturated fat.*

POLYUNSATURATED FATS

There are two types, those of vegetable or plant origin, such as sunflower oil, soft margarine and seeds (omega 6) and those from oily fish (omega 3). Both are usually liquid at room temperature.

At one time it was believed to be beneficial to switch to polyunsaturates as they may also help lower cholesterol. Today most experts believe that it's more important to reduce the total intake of all kinds of fat.

The Cholesterol Question

Cholesterol is a fat-like substance which plays a vital role in the body. It's the material from which many essential hormones and vitamin D are made. However, too much saturated fat encourages the body to make more cholesterol than it needs or can get rid of.

Cholesterol is carried around the body, attached to proteins called high density lipoproteins (HDL), low density lipoproteins (LDL), and very low density lipoproteins (VLDL or triglycerides). After eating, the LDLs carry the fat in the blood to the cells where it's required. Any surplus should be excreted from the body; however, if there is too much LDL in the blood, some of the fat will be deposited on the walls of the arteries. This scaling up gradually narrows the arteries and is one of the most common causes of heart attacks and strokes. In contrast, HDLs appear to protect against heart disease. Whether high triglyceride levels are risk factors remains unknown.

For some people, an excess of cholesterol in the blood is a hereditary trait; in others, it's mainly due to the consumption of too much saturated fat. In both cases though, it can be reduced by a low fat diet. Many people believe naturally high cholesterol foods such as egg yolks and organ meats should be avoided, but research has shown that it is more important to reduce total fat intake.

FATS & OILS		
Saturated	**Monounsaturated**	**Polyunsaturated**
Butter	Olive oil	Corn oil
Lard	Grapeseed oil	Safflower oil
Hard margarine	Rapeseed (Canola) oil	Soybean oil
Suet		Sunflower oil
Vegetarian suet		Walnut oil
Coconut oil		Soft margarines, labelled 'high in polyunsaturates'
Palm oil		

Eating a Healthy Low Fat Diet

Eat a good variety of different foods every day to make sure you get all the nutrients you need.

1 Skim milk contains the same amount of calcium, protein and B vitamins as whole milk, but a fraction of the fat.

2 Low-fat yogurt, cottage cheese and ricotta cheese are all high in calcium and protein, and are good substitutes for cream.

3 Starchy foods such as rice, bread, potatoes, cereals and pasta should be eaten at every meal. These foods provide energy and some vitamins, minerals and dietary fiber.

4 Vegetables, salads and fruits should form a major part of the diet, and about 1 lb should be eaten each day.

5 Eat meat in moderation but eat plenty of fish, particularly oily fish such as mackerel, salmon, tuna, herring and sardines.

A few simple changes to a normal diet can reduce fat intake considerably. The following tips are designed to make the change to a healthier diet as easy as possible.

Meat and poultry
Red meats such as lamb, pork and beef are high in saturated fats, but chicken and turkey contain far less fat. Remove the skin before cooking and trim off any visible fat. Avoid sausages, burgers, pâtés, bacon and minced beef. Buy lean cuts of meat and skim any fat from the surface of stocks and stews.

Dairy products
Replace whole milk with skim or 1% milk and use low-fat yogurt, low-fat sour cream or ricotta cheese instead of cream. Use cream, cream cheese and hard cheeses in moderation. There are reduced-fat cheeses on the market with 14% fat content which is half the fat content of full fat cheese. Use these wherever possible.

Spreads, oils and dressings
Use butter, margarine and low-fat spreads sparingly. Try to avoid using fat and oil for cooking. If you have to use oil, choose olive, corn, sunflower, canola and peanut oils, which are low in saturates. Look out for oil-free dressings and reduced-fat mayonnaise.

Hidden fats
Muffins, cakes, pastries, snacks, chips, and processed meals all contain high proportions of fat. Get into the habit of reading food labels carefully and looking for a low-fat option.

Cooking methods
Grill, poach and steam foods whenever possible. If you do fry foods, use as little fat as possible and pat off the excess after browning, with paper towels. Make sauces and stews by first cooking the onions and garlic in a small quantity of stock, rather than frying in oil.

A selection of foods for a healthy low-fat diet.

EASY WAYS TO CUT DOWN FAT AND SATURATED FAT

EAT LESS	TRY INSTEAD
Butter and hard fats.	Try spreading butter more thinly, or replace it with a low fat spread or polyunsaturated margarine.
Fatty meats and high fat products such as meat pies and sausages.	Buy the leanest cuts of meat you can afford and choose low fat meats like skinless chicken or turkey. Look for reduced fat sausages and meat products. Eat fish more often, especially oily fish.
Full fat dairy products like cream, butter, hard margarine, milk and hard cheeses.	Choose skim or 1% low fat milk and milk products, and try low fat yogurt, low fat fromage frais and lower fat cheeses such as skim milk cream cheese, reduced fat Cheddar, mozzarella or Brie.
Hard cooking fats such as lard or hard margarine.	Choose monounsaturated or polyunsaturated oils for cooking, such as olive, sunflower, corn or soybean oil.
Rich salad dressings like mayonnaise or cream dressing.	Make salad dressings with low fat yogurt or fromage frais, or use a healthy oil such as olive oil.
Fried foods.	Broil, microwave, steam or bake when possible. Roast meats on a rack. Fill up on starchy foods like pasta, rice and couscous. Choose baked or boiled potatoes, not fried.
Added fat in cooking.	Use heavy-based or non-stick pans so you can cook with little or no added fat.
High fat snacks such as chips, chocolate, cakes, pastries and cookies.	Choose fresh or dried fruit, breadsticks or vegetable sticks. Make your own low fat cakes and bakes.

Choosing a Chicken

When choosing a fresh chicken, it should have a plump breast and the skin should be creamy in color.

A bird's dressed weight is taken after plucking and drawing and may include the giblets (neck, gizzard, heart and liver). A frozen chicken must be thawed slowly and thoroughly in the refrigerator – never at room temperature. Rinse with cool water and pat dry with a paper towel. Always clean surfaces after preparing raw chicken and do not place cooked chicken where raw chicken has been.

Roasters
These birds are about six to twelve months old and weigh 3–4 lb. They will feed a family.

Spring chickens
These birds are about three months old and weigh from 2–2½ lb. They will serve three to four people.

Stewing hens
These are about twelve months and over and weigh between 4–6 lb. They require long, slow cooking, around 2–3 hours, to make them tender.

Free-range chickens
These corn-fed birds have a deeper yellow skin, and are generally more expensive. They usually weigh 2½–3 lb.

Broilers
These are eight to ten weeks old and weigh 1½–2 lb. They will serve two people. Broilers are best roasted, broiled or pot-roasted.

Poussins
These are four to six weeks old and weigh 1–1¼ lb. Rock Cornish game hens can be substituted if desired.

Cuts of Chicken

Today, chicken is available pre-packaged in a variety of different ways. If you do not want to buy a whole bird, you can choose from the many selected cuts on the market. Most cooking methods are suitable for all cuts, but some are especially suited to specific cuts of meat.

Leg
This comprises the thigh and drumstick. Large pieces with bones, such as this, are suitable for slow-cooking, such as casseroling or poaching.

Skinless boneless thigh
This makes tasks such as stuffing and rolling much quicker, as it is already skinned and jointed.

Liver
This makes a wonderful addition to pâtés or to salads.

Drumstick
The drumstick is a firm favorite for barbecuing or frying, either in batter or rolled in breadcrumbs.

Wing
The wing does not supply much meat, and is often barbecued or fried.

Breast
This comprises tender white meat and can be simply cooked in butter, as well as stuffed.

Minced chicken
This is not as strongly flavored as, say, ground beef, but may be used as a substitute in some recipes.

Thigh
The thigh is suitable for casseroling and other slow-cooking methods.

Tips for Reducing Fat

• Keep chicken meat tender by roasting with the skin on. Remove the skin before serving, for reduced fat benefits.

• Use a cooking method that needs little or no fat such as poaching, broiling, stir-frying, baking, grilling or roasting.

• Instead of making traditional gravy, skim off all the fat from the roasting pan and make a low fat gravy with the meat juices, herbs and chicken broth.

• When roasting chicken, add garlic to the roasting pan with the chicken, then purée the roasted garlic with the juices in the pan to make a tasty sauce without fat.

• Remove all the skin and any visible fat from chicken thighs, drumsticks and breasts before cooking (right).

REDUCE THE FAT, NOT THE FLAVOR

• Use chopped garlic, fresh herbs and spices to add flavor to skinned chicken before cooking. Rub the chosen ingredient into the chicken.

• Add a bouquet garni to stews or casseroles, if possible make it with a mixture of fresh herbs and tie them together with string, or use commercial bags of bouquet garni.

• Marinate in wine, cider, vinegar, lemon or lime juice. Skin and slash chicken pieces then pour over the marinade.

• Sprinkle finely chopped shallots, onions or scallions over the chicken, or if the chicken is whole, place a small whole onion in the cavity before cooking. Remove before serving.

• Before cooking, spread chicken breasts with prepared mustard to add a piquant flavor.

• Serve plain cooked chicken with a fruit or vegetable salsa. Make the salsa from any selection of finely chopped fruit or vegetables. Scallions and chopped fresh herbs such as cilantro or parsley add fresh flavor.

Low Fat Cooking Methods

• Oven bake chicken with vegetables and herbs in paper packages.

• Broiling – marinate first to add flavor. Fat drips off chicken during cooking.

• Steaming – this retains the moisture and needs no added fat. Add flavor boosters such as lemon rind, garlic and herbs, or steam over smoky-flavored tea.

• Baking – dip chicken breasts in egg white then in a light coating of rolled oats to produce tender chicken.

• Stir-fry in a small amount of hot oil in a wok – oil spreads further when hot, so less is needed. The chicken is then quickly sealed and doesn't absorb much oil.

• Poaching – poach skinless chicken pieces in broth with vegetables, then blend the cooked vegetables to make a delicious purée to serve with the chicken.

Chicken Roulades

These chicken rolls make a light lunch dish for two, or a starter for four. They can be sliced and served cold with a salad.

CALORIES 239
FAT 14.5 g **SATURATED FAT** 4.6 g
CHOLESTEROL 56.2 mg

Makes 4

INGREDIENTS
4 boned and skinned chicken thighs
4 oz chopped frozen spinach
1 tbsp butter
2 tbsp pine nuts
pinch of ground nutmeg
7 tbsp fresh white bread crumbs
4 rashers lean bacon
2 tbsp olive oil
⅔ cup white wine or fresh or canned chicken stock
2 tsp cornstarch
2 tbsp light cream
1 tbsp chopped fresh chives
salt and freshly ground black pepper

bread crumbs

bacon   spinach

butter

chives

pine nuts

olive oil

light cream

cornstarch   chicken thighs

1 Preheat the oven to 350°F. Place the chicken thighs between two sheets of plastic wrap and flatten with a rolling pin.

2 Put the spinach and butter into a saucepan, heat gently until the spinach has defrosted, then increase the heat and cook rapidly, stirring occasionally until all the moisture has evaporated. Add the pine nuts, seasoning, nutmeg and fresh bread crumbs.

3 Divide the filling between the chicken pieces and roll up neatly. Wrap a rasher of bacon around each piece and secure with string.

4 Heat the oil in a large frying pan and brown the rolls all over. Drain through a slotted spoon and place in a shallow ovenproof dish.

5 Pour over the wine or stock, cover, and bake for 15–20 minutes, or until tender. Transfer the chicken to a serving plate and remove the string. Strain the cooking liquid into a saucepan.

6 Mix the cornstarch to a smooth paste with a little cold water and add to the juices in the pan, along with the cream. Bring to a boil to thicken, stirring all the time. Adjust the seasoning and add the chives. Pour the sauce round the chicken and serve.

Spiced Chicken Livers

Chicken livers can be bought frozen, but make sure that you defrost them thoroughly before using. Serve as a first course or light meal along with a mixed salad and garlic bread.

Serves 4

INGREDIENTS
12 oz chicken livers
1 cup all-purpose flour
½ tsp ground coriander
½ tsp ground cumin
½ tsp ground cardamom seeds
¼ tsp ground paprika
¼ tsp ground nutmeg
6 tbsp olive oil
salt and freshly ground black pepper
garlic bread, to serve

chicken livers

olive oil

flour

coriander

cardamom seeds

cumin

paprika

nutmeg

1 Dry the chicken livers on paper towels, removing any unwanted pieces. Cut the large livers in half and leave the smaller ones whole.

2 Mix the flour with all the spices and the seasoning.

NUTRITIONAL NOTES
PER PORTION:

CALORIES 297
FAT 14.4 g **SATURATED FAT** 2.9 g
CHOLESTEROL 332.5 mg

3 Coat the first batch of livers with spiced flour, separating each piece. Heat the oil in a large frying pan and fry the livers in small batches. (This helps to keep the oil temperature high and prevents the flour from becoming soggy.)

4 Fry quickly, stirring frequently, until crispy. Keep warm and repeat with the remaining livers. Serve immediately with warm garlic bread.

Chicken Tikka

The red food coloring gives this dish its traditional bright color. Serve with lemon wedges and a crisp mixed salad.

Serves 4

INGREDIENTS

1 × 3½ lb chicken
mixed salad leaves, e.g. frisée and
   oakleaf lettuce or radicchio,
   to serve

FOR THE MARINADE

⅔ cup plain low fat yogurt
1 tsp ground paprika
2 tsp grated fresh ginger root
1 garlic clove, crushed
2 tsp garam masala
½ tsp salt
red food coloring (optional)
juice of 1 lemon

lemon

chicken

salt

yogurt

paprika

ginger

garlic

garam masala

1 Joint the chicken and cut it into eight pieces, using a sharp knife.

2 Mix all the marinade ingredients in a container large enough to hold the chicken pieces. Add the chicken, coat well and chill for 4 hours or overnight to allow the flavors to penetrate the flesh.

NUTRITIONAL NOTES

PER PORTION:

CALORIES 131
FAT 4.5 g **SATURATED FAT** 1.4 g
CHOLESTEROL 55.4 mg

3 Preheat the oven to 400°F. Remove the chicken pieces from the marinade and arrange them in a single layer in a large ovenproof dish. Bake for 30–40 minutes or until tender.

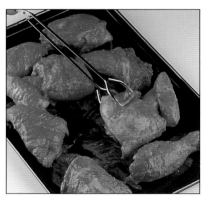

4 Baste with a little of the marinade while cooking. Arrange on a bed of salad leaves and serve hot or cold.

French Chicken Salad

A light first course for eight people or a substantial main course for four. Arrange attractively on individual plates to serve.

Serves 8

INGREDIENTS

1 × 3½ lb free-range chicken
1¼ cups white wine and water, mixed
24 × ¼ in slices French bread
1 garlic clove, peeled
8 oz green beans
4 oz fresh young spinach leaves
2 stalks celery, thinly sliced
2 scallions, thinly sliced
2 sun-dried tomatoes, chopped
fresh chives and parsley, to garnish

FOR THE VINAIGRETTE

2 tbsp red wine vinegar
6 tbsp olive oil
1 tbsp whole grain mustard
1 tbsp honey
2 tbsp chopped mixed fresh herbs, e.g. thyme, parsley and chives
2 tsp finely chopped capers
salt and freshly ground black pepper

honey

olive oil

free-range chicken

spinach

red wine vinegar

green beans

1 Preheat the oven to 375°F. Put the chicken into a casserole with the wine and water. Roast for 1½ hours until tender. Leave to cool in the liquid. Remove the skin and bones and cut the flesh into small pieces.

2 To make the vinaigrette, put all the ingredients into a screw-topped jar and shake vigorously to emulsify. Adjust the seasoning to taste.

3 Toast the French bread under the broiler or in the oven until dry and golden brown, then lightly rub with the peeled garlic clove.

4 Trim the green beans, cut into 2 in lengths and cook in boiling water until just tender (*al dente*). Drain and rinse under cold running water.

5 Wash the spinach thoroughly, remove the stalks and tear into small pieces. Arrange on serving plates with the sliced celery, green beans, scallions, chicken and sun-dried tomatoes.

20

NUTRITIONAL NOTES
PER PORTION:

CALORIES 306
FAT 9.9 g **SATURATED FAT** 2.3 g
CHOLESTEROL 54.9 mg

6 Spoon over the vinaigrette dressing. Arrange the toasted croûtons on top, garnish with extra fresh chives and parsley, if desired, and serve immediately.

Sesame Seed Chicken Bites

Best served warm, these crunchy bites are delicious accompanied by a glass of chilled dry white wine.

Makes 20

INGREDIENTS
6 oz raw chicken breast
2 cloves garlic, crushed
1 in piece ginger root, peeled
    and grated
1 medium egg white
1 tsp cornstarch
¼ cup shelled pistachios, roughly
    chopped
4 tbsp sesame seeds
2 tbsp grapeseed oil
salt and freshly ground black pepper

FOR THE SAUCE
¼ cup hoisin sauce
1 tbsp sweet chili sauce

TO GARNISH
ginger root, finely shredded
pistachios, roughly chopped
fresh dill sprigs

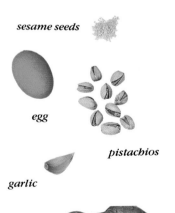

sesame seeds

egg

pistachios

garlic

ginger

1 Place the chicken, garlic, grated ginger, egg white and cornstarch into the food processor and process them to a smooth paste.

2 Stir in the pistachios and season well with salt and pepper.

NUTRITIONAL NOTES
PER PORTION:

CALORIES 53
FAT 4.1 g **SATURATED FAT** 0.2 g
CHOLESTEROL 3.8 mg

3 Roll into 20 balls and coat with sesame seeds. Heat the wok and add the oil. When the oil is hot, stir-fry the chicken bites in batches, turning regularly until golden. Drain on paper towels.

4 Make the sauce by mixing together the hoisin and chili sauces in a bowl. Garnish the bites with shredded ginger, pistachios and dill, then serve hot, with a dish of sauce for dipping.

Tandoori Chicken

Traditionally baked in a clay oven called a tandoor, this tasty dish can also be cooked in a conventional oven.

Serves 4

INGREDIENTS
4 chicken quarters
¾ cup low fat plain yogurt
1 teaspoon garam masala
1 teaspoon grated fresh ginger
1 garlic clove, crushed
1½ teaspoons chili powder
¼ teaspoon ground turmeric
1 teaspoon ground coriander
1 tablespoon lemon juice
1 teaspoon salt
few drops of red food coloring
2 tablespoons corn oil

FOR THE GARNISH
mixed greens
lime wedges

chicken

ginger

plain yogurt

garam masala

garlic

chili powder

turmeric

ground coriander

lemon juice

corn oil

1 Skin the chicken quarters, rinse them under cold water and pat them dry with paper towels. Make two slits into the flesh of each piece, place the pieces in a shallow dish and set aside.

2 Mix the yogurt, garam masala, ginger, garlic, chili powder, turmeric, ground coriander, lemon juice, salt, red coloring and oil in a bowl. Beat until the ingredients are thoroughly combined.

3 Cover the chicken quarters with the spice mixture and let marinate for about 3 hours.

4 Preheat the oven to 475°F. Transfer the chicken pieces to an ovenproof dish.

5 Bake for 20–25 minutes or until the chicken is cooked right through and browned on top.

6 Remove the dish from the oven, transfer the chicken pieces to a serving dish and garnish with the mixed greens and lime wedges.

NUTRITIONAL NOTES
PER PORTION:

CALORIES 242
FAT 10.6 g **SATURATED FAT** 2.7 g
CHOLESTEROL 81.9 mg

Italian Vegetable Soup

The success of this clear soup depends on the quality of the stock, so use homemade vegetable stock rather than bouillon cubes.

Serves 4

INGREDIENTS
1 small carrot
1 baby leek
1 celery stalk
2 oz green cabbage
3¾ cups vegetable
  stock
1 bay leaf
1 cup cooked cannellini beans, rinsed
  and drained
⅕ cup soup pasta, such as tiny shells,
  bows, stars or elbows
salt and freshly ground black pepper
snipped fresh chives, to garnish

stock

cabbage

bay leaf

chives

baby leek

celery

carrot

pasta

1 Cut the carrot, leek and celery into 2 in long julienne strips. Slice the cabbage very finely.

2 Put the stock and bay leaf into a large saucepan and bring to a boil. Add the carrot, leek and celery, cover and simmer for 6 minutes.

NUTRITIONAL NOTES

PER PORTION:

CALORIES 126
FAT 2.2 g **SATURATED FAT** 0.6 g
CHOLESTEROL 19 mg

3 Add the cabbage, beans and pasta shapes. Stir, then simmer uncovered for a further 4-5 minutes, or until the vegetables and pasta are tender.

4 Remove the bay leaf and season to taste. Ladle into four soup bowls and garnish with snipped chives. Serve immediately.

Corn and Chicken Soup

This popular classic Chinese soup is very easy to make.

Serves 4-6

INGREDIENTS
1 chicken breast fillet,
    about 4 oz, cubed
2 tsp light soy sauce
1 tbsp Chinese rice wine
1 tsp cornstarch
4 tbsp cold water
1 tsp sesame oil
2 tbsp peanut oil
1 tsp fresh ginger,
    finely grated
4 cups chicken stock, or
    bouillon cube and water
15-oz can cream-style corn
8-oz can corn kernels
2 eggs, beaten
2–3 scallions, green parts only,
    cut into tiny rounds
salt and ground black pepper

cornstarch

chicken stock

cream-style corn

chicken

Chinese rice wine

corn kernels

egg

sesame oil

ginger

NUTRITIONAL NOTES
PER PORTION:
CALORIES 163
FAT 4.6 g **SATURATED FAT** 1.0 g
CHOLESTEROL 72.4 mg

1 Grind the chicken in a food processor, taking care not to over-process. Transfer the chicken to a bowl and stir in the soy sauce, rice wine, cornstarch, water, sesame oil and seasoning. Cover and leave for about 15 minutes to absorb the flavors.

2 Heat a wok over medium heat. Add the peanut oil and swirl it around. Add the ginger and stir-fry for a few seconds. Add the stock, creamed corn and corn kernels. Bring to just below boiling point.

3 Spoon about 6 tbsp of the hot liquid into the chicken mixture and stir until it forms a smooth paste. Return this to the wok. Slowly bring to a boil, stirring constantly, then simmer for 2–3 minutes until the chicken is cooked.

4 Pour the beaten eggs into the soup in a slow steady stream, using a fork or chopsticks to stir the top of the soup in a figure-eight pattern. The egg should set in lacy shreds. Serve immediately with the scallions sprinkled over.

Warm Chicken Salad with Shallots and Snow Peas

Succulent cooked chicken pieces are combined with vegetables in a light chili dressing.

Serves 6

INGREDIENTS
2 ounces mixed greens
2 ounces baby spinach leaves
2 ounces watercress
2 tablespoons chili sauce
2 tablespoons dry sherry
1 tablespoon light soy sauce
1 tablespoon ketchup
2 teaspoons olive oil
8 shallots, finely chopped
1 garlic clove, crushed
12 ounces skinless, boneless
  chicken breast, cut into thin strips
1 red bell pepper, seeded
  and sliced
6 ounces snow peas, trimmed
14-ounce can baby corn,
  drained and halved
10 ounces brown rice
salt and ground black pepper
parsley sprig, to garnish

mixed greens

spinach

watercress

chili sauce

dry sherry

light soy sauce

ketchup

olive oil

shallots

garlic

chicken breasts

red bell pepper

snow peas

baby corn

brown rice

1 Arrange the mixed greens and the spinach leaves on a serving dish, tearing up any large leaves. Add the watercress and toss to mix.

2 In a small bowl, combine the chili sauce, sherry, soy sauce and ketchup and set aside.

3 Heat the oil in a large non-stick frying pan or wok. Add the shallots and garlic and stir-fry over medium heat for 1 minute.

4 Add the chicken and stir-fry for 3–4 minutes.

NUTRITIONAL NOTES
PER PORTION:
CALORIES 184
FAT 3.9 g **SATURATED FAT** 0.9 g
CHOLESTEROL 25.1 mg

COOK'S TIP

Use other lean meat such as turkey breast, beef or pork in place of the chicken.

5 Add the pepper, snow peas, corn and rice and stir-fry for 2–3 minutes.

6 Pour in the chili sauce mixture and stir-fry for 2–3 minutes, until hot and bubbling. Season to taste. Spoon the chicken mixture over the mixed greens, toss together and serve immediately, garnished with fresh parsley.

Curried Chicken Salad

Serves 4

INGREDIENTS

2 cooked chicken breasts, boned
6 ounces green beans
12 ounces multi-colored penne
²/₃ cup low-fat yogurt
1 teaspoon mild curry powder
1 garlic clove, crushed
1 green chili, seeded and
    finely chopped
2 tablespoons chopped
    fresh cilantro
4 firm ripe tomatoes, peeled, seeded
    and cut in strips
salt and ground black pepper
fresh cilantro leaves, to garnish

multi-colored penne

chicken breasts

green beans

green chili

cilantro

tomatoes

low-fat yogurt

garlic

NUTRITIONAL NOTES

PER PORTION:

CALORIES 449
FAT 5.1 g **SATURATED FAT** 1.3 g
CHOLESTEROL 38 mg

1 Remove the skin from the chicken and cut in strips. Cut the green beans in 1-inch lengths and cook in boiling water for 5 minutes. Drain and rinse under cold water.

2 Cook the pasta in a large pan of boiling, salted water until *al dente*. Drain and rinse thoroughly.

3 To make the sauce, mix the yogurt, curry powder, garlic, chilli and chopped cilantro together in a bowl. Stir in the chicken pieces and let stand for 30 minutes.

4 Transfer the pasta to a glass bowl and toss with the beans and tomatoes. Spoon over the chicken and sauce. Garnish with cilantro leaves.

Chicken and Pasta Salad

This is a delicious way to use up left-over cooked chicken, and makes a filling meal.

Serves 4

INGREDIENTS

8 oz tri-colored pasta twists
2 tbsp bottled pesto sauce
1 tbsp olive oil
1 beefsteak tomato
12 pitted black olives
8 oz cooked green beans
12 oz cooked chicken, cubed
salt and freshly ground black pepper
fresh basil, to garnish

tomato

pesto sauce

green beans

basil

olive oil

pasta twists

chicken

black olives

1 Cook the pasta in plenty of boiling, salted water until *al dente* (for about 12 minutes or as directed on the package).

2 Drain the pasta and rinse in plenty of cold running water. Put into a bowl and stir in the pesto sauce and olive oil.

NUTRITIONAL NOTES

PER PORTION:

CALORIES 416
FAT 13.9 g **SATURATED FAT** 3.1 g
CHOLESTEROL 67.9 mg

3 Skin the tomato by placing in boiling water for about 10 seconds and then into cold water, to loosen the skin.

4 Cut the tomato into small cubes and add to the pasta with the black olives, seasoning and green beans cut into 1 ½ in lengths. Add the cubed chicken. Toss gently together and transfer to a serving platter. Garnish with fresh basil.

Tex-Mex Chicken Salad

Serves 6

INGREDIENTS
1 teaspoon ground cumin seeds
1 teaspoon ground paprika
1 teaspoon ground turmeric
1–2 garlic cloves, crushed
2 tablespoons lime juice
4 chicken breasts, boned
   and skinned
8 ounces rigatoni
1 red bell pepper, chopped
2 stalks celery, sliced thinly
1 shallot or small onion,
   finely chopped
1 ounce stuffed green
   olives, halved
2 tablespoons honey
1 tablespoon coarse-grained mustard
1–2 tablespoons lime juice
salt and ground black pepper
mixed salad, to serve

chicken breasts

honey
cumin seeds
red bell pepper
onion
lime
turmeric   *garlic*
celery
mixed salad

rigatoni

stuffed olives

paprika

1 Mix the cumin, paprika, turmeric, garlic, seasoning and lime juice in a bowl. Rub this mixture over the chicken breasts. Lay in a shallow dish, cover with plastic wrap and refrigerate for about 3 hours or overnight.

2 Preheat the oven to 400°F. Put the chicken in an ovenproof dish in a single layer and bake for 20 minutes (or broil for 8–10 minutes on each side).

3 Cook the rigatoni in a large pan of boiling, salted water until *al dente*. Drain and rinse under cold water. Pat dry with paper towels.

4 Put the red pepper, celery, shallot or small onion and olives into a large bowl with the pasta.

5 Mix the honey, mustard and lime juice together in a bowl and pour over the pasta. Toss to coat.

6 Cut the chicken in bite-size pieces. Arrange the mixed salad leaves on a serving dish, spoon the pasta mixture in the center and top with the spicy chicken pieces.

NUTRITIONAL NOTES
PER PORTION:

CALORIES 277
FAT 5.6 g **SATURATED FAT** 1.4 g
CHOLESTEROL 49 mg

Dijon Chicken Salad

An attractive and elegant dish to serve for lunch
with herb and garlic bread.

Serves 4

INGREDIENTS
4 boned and skinned chicken breasts
mixed salad leaves, e.g. watercress
   and oakleaf lettuce, to serve

FOR THE MARINADE
2 tbsp Dijon mustard
3 garlic cloves, crushed
1 tbsp grated onion
4 tbsp white wine

FOR THE MUSTARD DRESSING
2 tbsp tarragon wine vinegar
1 tsp Dijon mustard
1 tsp honey
6 tbsp olive oil
salt and freshly ground black pepper

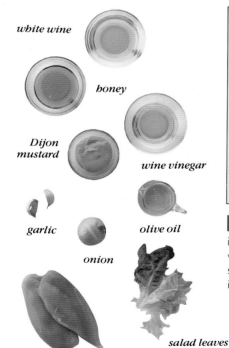

white wine

honey

Dijon mustard

wine vinegar

garlic

olive oil

onion

salad leaves

chicken breasts

1 Mix all the marinade ingredients together in a shallow glass or earthenware dish that is large enough to hold the chicken in a single layer.

2 Turn the chicken over in the marinade to coat completely, cover with plastic wrap and then chill in the refrigerator overnight.

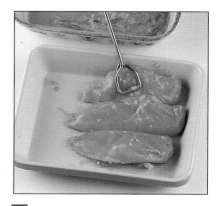

3 Preheat the oven to 375°F. Transfer the chicken and the marinade into an ovenproof dish, cover with foil and bake for about 35 minutes or until tender. Leave to cool in the liquid.

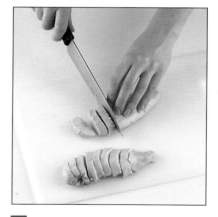

4 Put all the mustard dressing ingredients into a screw-topped jar, shake vigorously to emulsify, and adjust the seasoning. (This can be made several days in advance and stored in the refrigerator.)

5 Slice the chicken thinly, fan out the slices and arrange on a serving dish with the salad leaves.

6 Spoon over some of the mustard dressing and serve.

NUTRITIONAL NOTES
PER PORTION:

CALORIES 125
FAT 6.5 g **SATURATED FAT** 1.2 g
CHOLESTEROL 26.9 mg

Warm Stir-fried Salad

Warm salads are becoming increasingly popular because they are delicious and nutritious. Arrange the salad leaves on four individual plates, so the hot stir-fry can be served quickly on to them, ensuring the lettuce remains crisp and the chicken warm.

NUTRITIONAL NOTES

PER PORTION:

CALORIES 219
FAT 7.4 g **SATURATED FAT** 1.6 g
CHOLESTEROL 48.4 mg

Serves 4

INGREDIENTS
1 tbsp fresh tarragon
2 boneless, skinless chicken breasts, about 8 oz each
2 in piece ginger root, peeled and finely chopped
3 tbsp light soy sauce
1 tbsp sugar
1 tbsp sunflower oil
1 Napa cabbage
½ chicory lettuce, torn into bite-size pieces
1 cup unsalted cashews
2 large carrots, peeled and cut into fine strips
salt and freshly ground black pepper

chicken breast

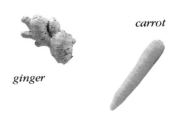
ginger

carrot

cashews

1 Chop the tarragon.

2 Cut the chicken into fine strips and place in a bowl.

3 To make the marinade, mix together in a bowl the tarragon, ginger, soy sauce, sugar and seasoning.

4 Pour the marinade over the chicken strips and leave for 2–4 hours.

5 Strain the chicken from the marinade. Heat the wok, then add the oil. When the oil is hot, stir-fry the chicken for 3 minutes, add the marinade and bubble for 2–3 minutes.

6 Slice the Napa cabbage and arrange on a plate with the chicory. Toss the cashews and carrots together with the chicken, pile on top of the bed of lettuce and serve immediately.

Grilled Chicken Salad with Lavender and Sweet Herbs

Lavender may seem like an odd salad ingredient, but its delightful scent has a natural affinity with sweet garlic, orange, and other wild herbs. A serving of cornmeal polenta makes this salad both filling and delicious.

Serves 4

INGREDIENTS
4 boneless chicken breasts
3¾ cups light chicken stock
1 cup fine polenta or cornmeal
2 oz butter
1 lb young spinach
6 oz lamb's lettuce
8 sprigs fresh lavender
8 small tomatoes, halved
salt and pepper

LAVENDER MARINADE
6 fresh lavender flowers
2 tsp finely grated orange zest
2 cloves garlic, crushed
2 tsp clear honey
salt
2 tbsp olive oil, French or Italian
2 tsp chopped fresh thyme
2 tsp chopped fresh marjoram

lavender   *chicken breasts*

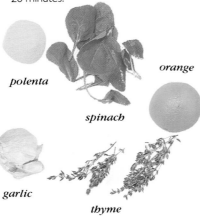

polenta

spinach

orange

garlic

thyme

1 To make the marinade, strip the lavender flowers from the stems and combine with the orange zest, garlic, honey, and salt. Add the olive oil and herbs. Score the chicken deeply, spread the mixture over the chicken, and leave to marinate in a cool place for at least 20 minutes.

2 To make the polenta, bring the chicken stock to a boil in a heavy saucepan. Add the cornmeal in a steady stream, stirring all the time until thick: this will take 2–3 minutes. Turn the cooked polenta out on to a 1-in-deep buttered tray and allow to cool.

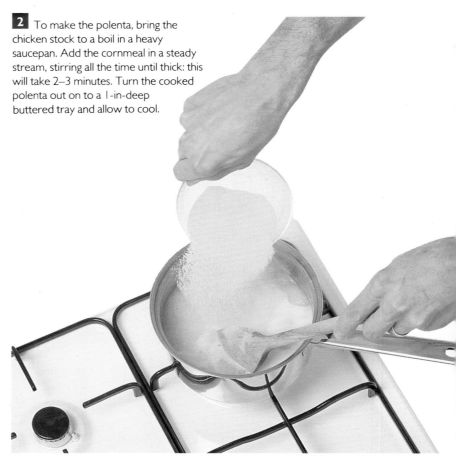

3 Heat the broiler to a moderate temperature. (If using a barbecue, let the embers settle to a steady glow.) Broil the chicken for 15 minutes, turning once.

4 Cut the polenta into 1 in cubes with a wet knife. Heat the butter in a large skillet and fry the polenta until golden.

COOK'S TIP

Lavender marinade is a delicious flavoring for fish as well as chicken. Try it over broiled cod, haddock, halibut, sea bass, and bream.

NUTRITIONAL NOTES

Per portion:

CALORIES 352
FAT 9.4 g **SATURATED FAT** 2.1g
CHOLESTEROL 43.3 mg

5 Wash the salad leaves and spin dry, then divide between 4 large plates. Slice each chicken breast and lay over the salad. Place the polenta among the salad, decorate with sprigs of lavender and tomatoes, season and serve.

Lemon Chicken Stir-fry

It is essential to prepare all the ingredients before you begin so they are ready to cook. This dish is cooked in minutes.

Serves 4

INGREDIENTS
4 boned and skinned chicken breasts
1 tbsp light soy sauce
5 tbsp cornstarch
1 bunch scallions
1 lemon
1 garlic clove, crushed
1 tbsp superfine sugar
2 tbsp sherry
2/3 cup fresh or canned chicken stock
4 tbsp olive oil
salt and freshly ground black pepper

NUTRITIONAL NOTES
PER PORTION:

CALORIES 298
FAT 9.9 g **SATURATED FAT** 2.1 g
CHOLESTEROL 53.8 mg

superfine sugar

garlic

olive oil

scallions

lemon

soy sauce

cornstarch

chicken breasts

1 Divide the chicken breasts into two natural fillets. Place each between two sheets of plastic wrap and flatten to a thickness of ¼ in with a rolling pin.

2 Cut into 1 in strips across the grain of the fillets. Put the chicken into a bowl with the soy sauce and toss to coat thoroughly, then sprinkle over 4 tbsp cornstarch to coat each piece.

3 Trim the roots off the scallions and cut diagonally into ½ in pieces. With a swivel peeler, remove the lemon rind in thin strips and cut into fine shreds. Reserve the lemon juice. Have ready the garlic clove, sugar, sherry, stock, lemon juice and the remaining cornstarch blended to a paste with cold water.

4 Heat the oil in a wok or large frying pan and cook the chicken very quickly in small batches for 3–4 minutes until lightly colored. Remove and keep warm while frying the rest of the chicken.

5 Add the scallions and garlic to the pan and cook for 2 minutes.

6 Add the remaining ingredients and bring to a boil, stirring until thickened. Add more sherry or stock if necessary and stir until the chicken is evenly covered with sauce. Reheat for 2 more minutes. Serve immediately.

Chicken Teriyaki

A bowl of boiled rice is the ideal accompaniment to this Japanese-style chicken dish.

Serves 4

INGREDIENTS
1 lb boneless, skinless chicken breasts

FOR THE MARINADE
1 tsp sugar
1 tbsp sake or rice wine
1 tbsp rice wine or dry sherry
2 tbsp dark soy sauce
rind of 1 orange, grated
orange segments and cress,
   to garnish

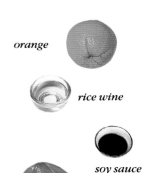

orange

rice wine

soy sauce

chicken breast

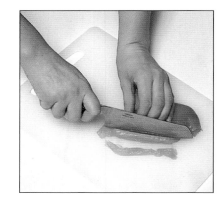

1 Finely slice the chicken.

2 Mix all the marinade ingredients together in a bowl.

3 Place the chicken in a bowl, pour over the marinade and leave to marinate for 15 minutes.

4 Heat the wok, add the chicken and marinade and stir-fry for 4–5 minutes. Serve garnished with orange segments and cress.

NUTRITIONAL NOTES
PER PORTION:

CALORIES 156
FAT 3.7 g **SATURATED FAT** 1.2 g
CHOLESTEROL 48.4 mg

COOK'S TIP
Make sure the marinade is brought to a boil and cooked for 4–5 minutes, because it has been in contact with raw chicken.

Chicken with Olives

If you use a nonstick pan you can cook these chicken cutlets in a minimum of oil.

Serves 4

INGREDIENTS
4 boned and skinned
  chicken breasts
¼ teaspoon cayenne pepper
1–2 tablespoons extra virgin
  olive oil
1 garlic clove, finely chopped
16–24 pitted black olives
6 ripe plum tomatoes, chopped
small handful fresh basil leaves

plum tomatoes

chicken

cayenne pepper

olive oil

garlic

pitted black olives

1 Carefully remove the fillets (the long finger-shaped muscle on the back of each breast) and reserve for another use.

2 Place each chicken breast between two sheets of plastic wrap and flatten with a rolling pin to a thickness of about ½ inch. Season with the cayenne.

3 Heat 1 tablespoon of the olive oil in a nonstick frying pan over high heat. Add the chicken and sear on both sides. Lower the heat and cook for 4–5 minutes until golden brown and just tender, turning them once. Using tongs, transfer the chicken to warmed serving plates. Keep hot while you cook the tomatoes and olives.

4 Reheat the oil in the pan (adding a little more if necessary) and fry the garlic for 1 minute until golden. Stir in the olives, cook for another minute. Stir in the tomatoes. Shred the basil and add to the olive and tomato mixture, spoon the sauce over the chicken and serve.

NUTRITIONAL NOTES

Per portion:

CALORIES 204
FAT 85.4 g **SATURATED FAT** 1.9 g
CHOLESTEROL 53.8 mg

Chicken with Cashews

This hot and spicy Indian dish has a deliciously thick and nutty sauce, and is best served with plenty of plain boiled rice.

Serves 6

INGREDIENTS

2 onions
2 tablespoons tomato paste
½ cup cashews
1½ teaspoons garam masala
1 garlic clove, crushed
1 teaspoon chili powder
1 tablespoon lemon juice
¼ teaspoon ground turmeric
1 teaspoon salt
1 tablespoon low fat plain yogurt
1 tablespoon corn oil
1 tablespoon chopped fresh
  cilantro, plus extra to
  garnish
1 tablespoon golden raisins
1 pound boned and skinned
  chicken breasts, cubed
1½ cups button mushrooms, halved
1¼ cups water

chili powder

lemon juice

button mushrooms

turmeric

onion

garlic

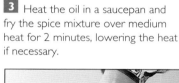
plain yogurt

garam masala

corn oil

fresh cilantro

cashews

chicken

golden raisins

1 Cut the onions into quarters and place in a food processor or blender. Process for about 1 minute.

2 Add the tomato paste, cashews, garam masala, garlic, chili powder, lemon juice, turmeric, salt and yogurt to the onions. Process for 1–1½ more minutes.

3 Heat the oil in a saucepan and fry the spice mixture over medium heat for 2 minutes, lowering the heat if necessary.

4 Add the cilantro, golden raisins and chicken and stir-fry for 1 minute more.

5 Add the mushrooms, pour in the water and bring to a simmer. Cover the pan and cook over low heat for about 10 minutes.

6 After this time, check that the chicken is cooked through and the sauce is thick. Cook for a little longer if necessary. Garnish with chopped fresh cilantro and serve.

NUTRITIONAL NOTES

PER PORTION:

CALORIES 187
FAT 9.8 g **SATURATED FAT** 1.9 g
CHOLESTEROL 43.2 mg

Chicken in Spicy Yogurt

Plan this dish well in advance; the extra-long marinating time is necessary to develop a really mellow spicy flavor.

NUTRITIONAL NOTES

PER PORTION:

CALORIES 158
FAT 5.1 g **SATURATED FAT** 1.6 g
CHOLESTEROL 58 mg

Serves 6

INGREDIENTS
6 chicken pieces
juice of 1 lemon
1 teaspoon salt

FOR THE MARINADE
1 teaspoon coriander seeds
2 teaspoons cumin seeds
6 cloves
2 bay leaves
1 onion, quartered
2 garlic cloves
2-inch piece fresh ginger, peeled and
 coarsely chopped
½ teaspoon chili powder
1 teaspoon turmeric
⅔ cup plain yogurt
lemon or lime and cilantro, to garnish

lemon

yogurt

coriander seeds

ginger

onion

garlic

bay leaves

chili powder

turmeric

cloves

cumin seeds

1 Skin the chicken joints and make deep slashes in the fleshiest parts with a sharp knife. Sprinkle over the lemon and salt and rub in.

2 Spread the coriander and cumin seeds, cloves and bay leaves in the bottom of a large frying pan and dry-fry over a moderate heat until the bay leaves are crispy.

3 Cool the spices and grind coarsely with a mortar and pestle.

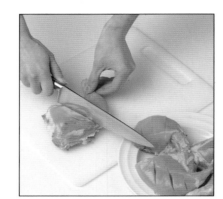

4 Finely mince the onion, garlic and ginger in a food processor or blender. Add the ground spices, chili, turmeric and yogurt, then strain in the lemon juice from the chicken.

5 Arrange the chicken in a single layer in a roasting tin. Pour over the marinade, then cover and chill for 24–36 hours.

6 Occasionally turn the chicken pieces in the marinade. Preheat the oven to 400°F. Cook the chicken for 45 minutes. Serve hot or cold, garnished with lemon or lime and cilantro leaves.

Spicy Chicken with Mint

For this tasty dish, the chicken is boiled before being quickly stir-fried in a little oil, to ensure that it is cooked through.

Serves 4

INGREDIENTS
10 ounces boned and skinned
   chicken breast, cut into strips
1¼ cups water
1 tablespoon corn oil
2 small bunches of scallions,
   roughly chopped
2 teaspoons chopped fresh ginger
1 teaspoon crumbled dried red chili
2 tablespoons lemon juice
1 tablespoon chopped
   fresh cilantro
1 tablespoon chopped fresh mint
3 tomatoes, seeded and
   roughly chopped
1 teaspoon salt
mint and cilantro sprigs, to garnish

1 Put the chicken and water in a saucepan, bring to a boil and lower the heat to medium. Cook for about 10 minutes or until the water has evaporated and the chicken is tender. Remove from the heat and set aside.

2 Heat the oil in a large non-stick frying pan or saucepan and stir-fry the scallions for about 2 minutes, until soft.

chicken

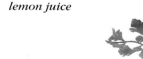
scallions

corn oil

fresh ginger

lemon juice

fresh cilantro

tomatoes

fresh mint

NUTRITIONAL NOTES
Per portion:

CALORIES 155
FAT 8.2 g **SATURATED FAT** 1.6 g
CHOLESTEROL 30.4 mg

3 Drain the cooked chicken strips and add them to the pan. Stir-fry for about 3 minutes over medium heat.

4 Gradually add the ginger, dried chili, lemon juice, fresh cilantro and mint, tomatoes and salt. Toss over the heat to warm the tomatoes through and let the flavors blend. Transfer to a serving dish and garnish with the fresh mint and cilantro sprigs.

Fragrant Chicken Curry

In this dish, the spiced sauce is thickened using lentils rather than the traditional onions fried in butter.

Serves 4

INGREDIENTS
½ cup red lentils
2 tablespoons mild curry powder
2 teaspoons ground coriander
1 teaspoon cumin seeds
2 cups vegetable broth
8 chicken thighs, skinned
8 ounces fresh shredded, or frozen
   spinach, thawed and well drained
1 tablespoon chopped fresh cilantro
salt and freshly ground black pepper
sprigs of fresh cilantro, to garnish
white or brown basmati rice and
   broiled papadums, to serve

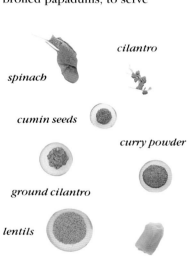

cilantro

spinach

cumin seeds

curry powder

ground cilantro

lentils

chicken thigh

1 Rinse the lentils under cold running water. Put into a large, heavy-based saucepan with the curry powder, ground coriander, cumin seeds and stock.

2 Bring to a boil then lower the heat. Cover and gently simmer for 10 minutes.

3 Add the chicken and spinach. Re-cover and simmer gently for a further 40 minutes, or until the chicken has cooked.

4 Stir in the chopped cilantro and season to taste. Serve garnished with fresh cilantro and accompanied by the rice and broiled papadums.

Grilled Chicken with Pica de Gallo Salsa

This dish originates from Mexico. Its hot fruity flavors form the essence of Tex-Mex Cooking.

NUTRITIONAL NOTES
PER PORTION:
CALORIES 197
FAT 7.1 g **SATURATED FAT** 1.7 g
CHOLESTEROL 53.8 mg

Serves 4

INGREDIENTS
4 chicken breasts
pinch of celery salt and cayenne
    pepper combined
2 tbsp vegetable oil
corn chips, to serve

FOR THE SALSA
10 oz watermelon
6 oz canteloupe melon
1 small red onion
1–2 green chilies
2 tbsp lime juice
4 tbsp chopped fresh cilantro
pinch of salt

green chilies

chicken breasts

red onion

lime

cilantro

canteloupe melon

watermelon

1 Preheat a moderate broiler. Slash the chicken breasts deeply to speed up the cooking time.

2 Season the chicken with celery salt and cayenne, brush with oil and broil for about 15 minutes.

3 To make the salsa, remove the rind and as many seeds as you can from the melons. Finely dice the flesh and put it into a bowl.

4 Finely chop the onion, split the chilies (discarding the seeds which contain most of the heat) and chop. Take care not to touch sensitive skin areas when handling cut chilies. Mix with the melon.

5 Add the lime juice and chopped cilantro, and season with a pinch of salt. Turn the salsa into a small bowl.

6 Arrange the grilled chicken on a plate and serve with the salsa and a handful of corn chips.

Chicken Liver Stir-fry

The final sprinkling of lemon, parsley and garlic granita gives this dish a delightful fresh flavor and wonderful aroma.

Serves 4

INGREDIENTS
1¼ lb chicken livers
6 tbsp butter
6 oz field mushrooms
2 oz chanterelle mushrooms
3 cloves garlic, finely chopped
2 shallots, finely chopped
⅔ cup medium sherry
3 fresh rosemary sprigs
2 tbsp fresh parsley, chopped
rind of 1 lemon, grated
salt and freshly ground pepper
fresh rosemary sprigs, to garnish
4 thick slices of white toast, to serve

1 Clean and trim the chicken livers to remove any gristle or muscle.

2 Season the livers generously with salt and freshly ground black pepper, tossing well to coat thoroughly.

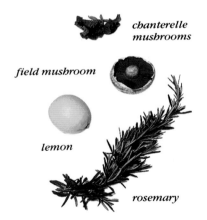

chanterelle mushrooms

field mushroom

lemon

rosemary

3 Heat the wok and add 1 tbsp of the butter. When melted, add the livers in batches (melting more butter where necessary but reserving 2 tbsp for the vegetables) and flash-fry until golden brown. Drain with a slotted spoon and transfer to a plate, then place in a low oven to keep warm.

4 Cut the field mushrooms into thick slices and, depending on the size of the chanterelles, cut in half.

5 Heat the wok and add the remaining butter. When melted, stir in two-thirds of the chopped garlic and the shallots and stir-fry for 1 minute until golden brown. Stir in the mushrooms and continue to cook for a further 2 minutes.

NUTRITIONAL NOTES

PER PORTION:

CALORIES 277
FAT 13.7 g **SATURATED FAT** 3.2 g
CHOLESTEROL 475 mg

6 Add the sherry, bring to a boil and simmer for 2–3 minutes until syrupy. Add the rosemary, salt and pepper and return livers to the pan. Stir-fry for 1 minute. Garnish with extra sprigs of rosemary, and serve sprinkled with a mixture of lemon, parsley and the remaining chopped garlic, with slices of toast.

Chicken and Bean Casserole

A delicious combination of chicken, fresh tarragon and mixed beans, topped with a layer of tender potatoes.

Serves 6

INGREDIENTS
2 pounds potatoes
½ cup reduced-fat aged
  Cheddar cheese, finely grated
2½ cups skim milk, plus
  2–3 tablespoons skim milk
2 tablespoons snipped
  fresh chives
2 leeks, washed and sliced
1 onion, sliced
2 tablespoons dry white wine
3 tablespoons low fat spread
⅓ cup whole wheat flour
1¼ cups chicken broth, cooled
12 ounces cooked skinless
  chicken breast, diced
3 cups brown cap
  mushrooms, sliced
11-ounce can red
  kidney beans
14-ounce can lima beans
14-ounce can black-eyed peas
2–3 tablespoons chopped
  fresh tarragon
salt and ground black pepper

potatoes

reduced-fat aged Cheddar cheese

skim milk

fresh chives

leeks

onion

cooked chicken breasts

dry white wine

low fat spread

whole wheat flour

chicken broth

lima beans

black-eyed peas

brown cap mushrooms

red kidney beans

fresh tarragon

1 Preheat the oven to 400°F. Cut the potatoes into chunks and cook in lightly salted, boiling water for 15–20 minutes, until tender. Drain thoroughly and mash. Add the cheese, 2–3 tablespoons milk and chives, season to taste and mix well. Keep warm and set aside.

2 Meanwhile, put the leeks and onion in a saucepan with the wine. Cover and cook gently for 10 minutes, until the vegetables are just tender, stirring occasionally.

3 In the meantime, put the low fat spread, flour, remaining milk and broth in a saucepan. Heat gently, whisking continuously, until the sauce comes to a boil and thickens. Simmer gently for 3 minutes, stirring.

4 Remove the pan from the heat and add the leek mixture, chicken and mushrooms and mix well.

5 Add all the rinsed and drained beans to the sauce and stir in with the tarragon and seasoning. Heat gently until the chicken mixture is piping hot, stirring.

COOK'S TIP

Sweet potatoes in place of standard potatoes work just as well in this recipe, and turkey or lean ham can be used in place of the chicken for a change.

6 Transfer it to an ovenproof dish and spoon or pipe the potato mixture over the top, to cover the chicken mixture completely. Bake for about 30 minutes, until the potato topping is crisp and golden brown. Serve immediately.

NUTRITIONAL NOTES

Per portion:

CALORIES 445
FAT 8.9 g **SATURATED FAT** 1.9 g
CHOLESTEROL 50.4 mg

Tuscan Chicken

This simple peasant casserole has all the flavors of traditional Italian ingredients.

Serves 4

INGREDIENTS
1 teaspoon olive oil
8 skinned chicken thighs
1 onion, thinly sliced
2 red bell peppers, seeded
  and sliced
1 garlic clove, crushed
1¼ cups crushed tomatoes
⅔ cup dry white wine
1 large fresh oregano sprig, or
  1 teaspoon dried oregano
14-ounce can cannellini
  beans, drained
3 tablespoons white bread crumbs
salt and ground black pepper

chicken thighs

olive oil

onion

red bell peppers

oregano sprig

cannellini
beans

fresh
bread crumbs

dry white wine

garlic

1 Heat the oil in a nonstick frying pan and fry the chicken until golden brown. Remove with a slotted spoon and keep hot. Add the onion and peppers to the pan and sauté gently, until softened, but not brown. Stir in the garlic.

2 Add the chicken, crushed tomatoes, wine and oregano. Season well, then bring to a boil with the lid on.

NUTRITIONAL NOTES
PER PORTION:

CALORIES 248
FAT 7.5 g **SATURATED FAT** 2.1 g
CHOLESTEROL 73 mg

3 Lower the heat and simmer gently, without a lid, for 30–35 minutes or until the chicken is tender and cooked through. Stir occasionally.

4 Stir in the cannellini beans and simmer for 5 minutes more to heat through. Sprinkle evenly with the bread crumbs and put under the broiler until golden brown.

Oat-crusted Chicken with Sage

Oats make a good coating for savory foods, and sealing in the natural juices means that you do not need to add extra fat.

Serves 4

INGREDIENTS
3 tablespoons skim milk
2 teaspoons mustard powder
½ cup rolled oats
3 tablespoons chopped sage leaves
8 skinned chicken thighs or
   drumsticks
½ cup low fat cream
1 teaspoon wholegrain mustard
salt and ground black pepper
fresh sage leaves, to garnish

skim milk

mustard powder

rolled oats

sage leaves

chicken thighs

low fat cream

wholegrain mustard

1 Preheat the oven to 400°F. Mix the milk and mustard powder in a cup. Mix the oats with 2 tablespoons of the sage in a shallow dish. Add salt and pepper to taste. Brush the chicken with the mustard and milk mixture and press into the oats to coat evenly.

2 Place the chicken on a baking sheet and bake for about 40 minutes or until the juices run clear, not pink, when pierced through the thickest part.

3 Meanwhile, mix the low fat cream, mustard and remaining sage. Season to taste. Garnish with fresh sage and serve hot or cold, with the sauce.

COOK'S TIP
If fresh sage is not available, use another fresh herb such as thyme or parsley instead of a dried alternative.

NUTRITIONAL NOTES
PER PORTION:

CALORIES 214
FAT 6.6 g **SATURATED FAT** 1.8 g
CHOLESTEROL 64.6 mg

Country Chicken Casserole

Succulent chicken joints in a vegetable sauce are excellent served with brown rice or pasta.

NUTRITIONAL NOTES
PER PORTION:

CALORIES 377
FAT 11.7 g **SATURATED FAT** 2.9 g
CHOLESTEROL 76.1 mg

Serves 4

INGREDIENTS
2 chicken breasts, skinned
2 chicken legs, skinned
2 tablespoons whole wheat flour
1 tablespoon sunflower oil
1¼ cups chicken broth
1¼ cups white wine
2 tablespoons crushed tomatoes
1 tablespoon tomato paste
4 strips lean bacon
1 large onion, sliced
1 garlic clove, crushed
1 green bell pepper, seeded
  and sliced
3 cups button mushrooms
8 ounces carrots, sliced
1 bouquet garni
8 ounces frozen Brussels sprouts
1½ cups frozen peas
salt and ground black pepper

1 Preheat the oven to 350°F. Coat the chicken pieces with seasoned flour.

2 Heat the oil in a large flameproof casserole, add the chicken and cook until browned all over. Remove the chicken using a slotted spoon and keep warm.

3 Add any remaining flour to the pan and cook for 1 minute. Gradually stir in the broth and wine, then add the crushed tomatoes and tomato paste.

chicken breasts and legs

whole wheat flour

sunflower oil

chicken broth

dry white wine

crushed tomatoes

tomato paste

bacon

onion

garlic

green bell pepper

button mushrooms

carrots

bouquet garni

Brussels sprouts

peas

4 Bring to a boil, stirring continuously, then add the chicken, bacon, onion, garlic, pepper, mushrooms, carrots and bouquet garni and stir. Cover and bake for 1½ hours, stirring once or twice.

COOK'S TIP
Use fresh Brussels sprouts and peas if available, and use red wine in place of white for a change.

5 Stir in the Brussels sprouts and peas, re-cover and bake for 30 more minutes.

6 Remove and discard the bouquet garni. Add seasoning to the casserole, garnish with chopped fresh parsley and serve immediately.

Chicken and Apricot Filo Pie

Filo is the low fat cook's best friend, as it contains little fat and needs only a light brushing of melted butter to create a crisp crust.

Serves 6

INGREDIENTS
½ cup bulgur wheat
½ cup boiling water
2 tablespoons butter
1 onion, chopped
1 pound lean ground chicken
¼ cup ready-to-eat dried
 apricots, finely chopped
¼ cup almonds, chopped
1 teaspoon ground cinnamon
½ teaspoon ground allspice
¼ cup low fat plain yogurt
1 tablespoon snipped fresh chives
2 tablespoons chopped fresh parsley
10 large sheets of filo pastry
salt and ground black pepper
chives, to garnish

NUTRITIONAL NOTES
PER PORTION:

CALORIES 239
FAT 6.3 g **SATURATED FAT** 1.6 g
CHOLESTEROL 43.0 mg

1 Preheat the oven to 400°F. Put the bulgur wheat in a bowl and add the boiling water. Let soak for 5–10 minutes, until all the water is absorbed.

2 Heat one tablespoon of the butter in a nonstick pan, and gently fry the onion and chicken until pale golden.

3 Stir in the apricots, almonds and bulgur. Cook for 2 more minutes. Remove from the heat and stir in the cinnamon, allspice, plain yogurt, chives and parsley. Season to taste with salt and pepper.

4 Melt the remaining butter. Cut the filo pastry into 10-inch rounds. Cover the pastry rounds with a cloth.

onion

bulgur wheat

ground
allspice

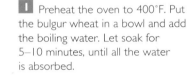
dried apricots

ground
cinnamon

ground
chicken

low fat plain yogurt

chives

filo pastry

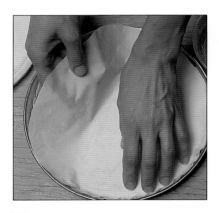

5 Line a 9 inch loose-based tart pan with three of the pastry rounds, brushing each one lightly with butter as you layer them. Spoon in the chicken mixture, then cover with three more rounds, brushed with butter as before.

6 Crumple the remaining rounds and place them on top of the pie, then brush with melted butter. Bake for about 30 minutes, until golden brown and crisp. Serve the pie hot or cold, cut in wedges and garnished with chives.

Crispy Spring Chickens

These small birds are about 2–2½ lb in weight and are delicious either hot or cold.

Serves 4

INGREDIENTS
2 × 2–2½ lb chickens
salt and freshly ground black pepper

FOR THE HONEY GLAZE
2 tbsp honey
2 tbsp sherry
1 tbsp vinegar

sherry

vinegar

honey

chicken

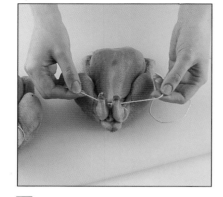

1 Preheat the oven to 350°F. Tie the birds into a neat shape and place on a wire rack over the sink. Pour over boiling water to plump the flesh and pat dry with paper towels.

2 Mix the honey, sherry and vinegar together and brush over the birds. Season with salt and pepper.

NUTRITIONAL NOTES

PER PORTION:

CALORIES 135
FAT 4.3 g **SATURATED FAT** 1.4 g
CHOLESTEROL 56.3 mg

3 Place the rack into a roasting pan and bake the birds for 45–55 minutes. Baste well with the honey glaze until crisp and golden brown.

Chicken in Herb Crusts

The chicken breasts can be brushed with melted butter instead of mustard before being coated in the bread crumb mixture. Serve with new potatoes and salad.

Serves 4

INGREDIENTS
4 boned and skinned chicken breasts
1 tbsp Dijon mustard
1 cup fresh bread crumbs
2 tbsp chopped fresh parsley
1 tbsp dried mixed herbs
2 tbsp butter, melted
salt and freshly ground black pepper

parsley

bread crumbs

Dijon mustard

chicken breasts

dried herbs

1 Preheat the oven to 350°F. Lay the chicken breasts in a greased ovenproof dish and spread them evenly with the Dijon mustard. Season with salt and freshly ground black pepper.

2 Mix the bread crumbs and herbs together thoroughly.

3 Press onto the chicken to coat. Spoon over the melted butter. Bake uncovered for 20 minutes or until tender and crisp.

NUTRITIONAL NOTES
PER PORTION:

CALORIES 217
FAT 7.9 g **SATURATED FAT** 1.9 g
CHOLESTEROL 54.0 mg

Chicken Bobotie

Perfect for a buffet party, this mild curry dish is set with savory custard, which makes serving easy. Serve with boiled rice and chutney.

NUTRITIONAL NOTES

PER PORTION:

CALORIES 334
FAT 12.8 g **SATURATED FAT** 3.1 g
CHOLESTEROL 138 mg

Serves 8

INGREDIENTS
two thick slices white bread
1⅞ cups milk
2 tbsp olive oil
2 medium onions, finely chopped
2½ tbsp medium curry powder
2½ lb ground raw chicken
1 tbsp apricot jam, chutney or
    superfine sugar
2 tbsp wine vinegar or lemon juice
3 large eggs, beaten
⅓ cup raisins or sultanas
12 whole almonds
salt and freshly ground black pepper

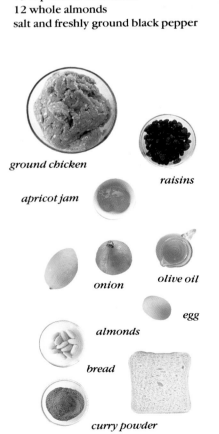

ground chicken

raisins

apricot jam

onion

olive oil

egg

almonds

bread

curry powder

1 Preheat the oven to 350°F. Soak the bread in ⅔ cup of the milk. Heat the oil in a frying pan and gently fry the onions until tender. Add the curry powder and continue to cook, stirring occasionally, for a further 2 minutes.

2 Add the ground chicken and brown all over, separating the grains of meat as they brown. Remove from the heat, season with salt and freshly ground black pepper, add the apricot jam, chutney or sugar and vinegar or lemon juice.

3 Mash the bread in the milk and add to the pan together with one of the beaten eggs and the raisins.

4 Grease a 2½ pint shallow ovenproof dish with butter. Spoon in the chicken mixture and level the top. Cover with buttered foil and bake for 30 minutes.

5 Meanwhile, beat the remaining eggs with the rest of the milk. Remove the dish from the oven and lower the temperature to 300°F. Break up the meat using two forks and pour over the beaten egg mixture.

6 Scatter the almonds over the top and return to the oven to bake, uncovered, for 30 minutes until set and golden brown all over.

Piquant Chicken with Spaghetti

Serves 4

INGREDIENTS

1 onion, finely chopped
1 carrot, diced
1 garlic clove, crushed
1¼ cups vegetable stock or water
4 small chicken breasts, boned and skinned
bouquet garni (bay leaf, parsley and thyme)
4 ounces button mushrooms, sliced thinly
1 teaspoon wine vinegar or lemon juice
12 ounces spaghetti
½ cucumber, peeled and sliced lengthwise
2 firm ripe tomatoes, peeled, seeded and chopped
2 tablespoons low-fat sour cream
1 tablespoon chopped fresh parsley
1 tablespoon snipped chives
salt and ground black pepper

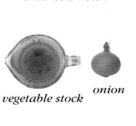

carrot

chicken breasts *tomatoes*

cucumber
chives

spaghetti
parsley

thyme

button mushrooms *bay leaf*

vegetable stock *onion*

1 Put the onion, carrot, garlic, stock or water into a saucepan with the chicken breasts and bouquet garni. Bring to a boil, cover and simmer gently for 15–20 minutes or until tender. Transfer the chicken to a plate and cover with foil.

2 Remove the chicken and strain the liquid. Discard the vegetables and return the liquid to the pan. Add the sliced mushrooms, wine vinegar or lemon juice and simmer for 2–3 minutes until tender.

3 Cook the spaghetti in a large pan of boiling, salted water until *al dente*. Drain thoroughly.

4 Blanch the cucumber in boiling water for 10 seconds. Drain and rinse under cold water.

5 Cut the chicken breasts into bite-size pieces. Boil the stock to reduce by half, then add the chicken, tomatoes, sour cream, cucumber and herbs. Season with salt and pepper to taste.

6 Transfer the spaghetti to a warmed serving dish and spoon over the piquant chicken. Serve at once.

NUTRITIONAL NOTES

PER PORTION:

CALORIES 472
FAT 7.6 g **SATURATED FAT** 2.5 g
CHOLESTEROL 65 mg

Chicken and Bean Risotto

Brown rice, red kidney beans, corn and broccoli add fiber to this healthy chicken dish.

Serves 4–6

INGREDIENTS
1 onion, chopped
2 garlic cloves, crushed
1 fresh red chili, seeded and
   finely chopped
2¼ cups mushrooms, sliced
2 stalks celery, chopped
1 cup long grain brown rice
1⅞ cups chicken broth
⅔ cup white wine
8 ounces skinless chicken
   breast, diced
14-ounce can red kidney
   beans
7-ounce can corn kernels
⅔ cup golden raisins
6 ounces small broccoli florets
2–3 tablespoons chopped fresh
   mixed herbs
salt and ground black pepper

onion
garlic
red chili
celery
mushrooms
long grain
brown rice
chicken
broth
dry white
wine
chicken
breasts
red kidney beans

corn
golden
raisins
broccoli
fresh mixed
herbs

1 Put the onion, garlic, chili, mushrooms, celery, rice, broth and wine in a saucepan. Cover, bring to a boil and simmer for 15 minutes.

2 Stir in the chicken, kidney beans, corn and golden raisins. Cook for 20 more minutes, until almost all the liquid has been absorbed.

NUTRITIONAL NOTES
PER PORTION:
CALORIES 353
FAT 4.3 g **SATURATED FAT** 1.1 g
CHOLESTEROL 28.1 mg

3 Meanwhile, cook the broccoli in boiling water for 5 minutes, then drain thoroughly.

4 Stir in the broccoli and chopped herbs, season to taste and serve immediately.

COOK'S TIP
Use 1 teaspoon hot chili powder in place of the fresh chili.

Chili Chicken Couscous

Don't neglect couscous. It provides one of the tastiest ways of adding bulk to a low-fat dish.

Serves 4

INGREDIENTS

2 cups couscous
4 cups boiling water
1 teaspoon olive oil
14 ounces boned and skinned
  chicken portions, diced
1 yellow bell pepper, seeded
  and sliced
2 large zucchini, thickly sliced
1 small fresh green chili, thinly
  sliced, or 1 teaspoon chili sauce
1 large tomato, diced
15-ounce can chick-peas, drained
salt and ground black pepper
fresh cilantro sprigs, to garnish

1 Place the couscous in a large bowl and pour over the boiling water. Cover and let stand for 30 minutes.

chicken

olive oil

yellow bell pepper

tomato

chick-peas

couscous

cilantro sprig

green chili

zucchini

NUTRITIONAL NOTES
Per portion:

CALORIES 363
FAT 8.1 g **SATURATED FAT** 1.7 g
CHOLESTEROL 57 mg

2 Heat the oil in a large, nonstick pan. Stir-fry the chicken quickly to seal, then reduce the heat. Stir in the pepper, zucchini and chili. Cook for 10 minutes, until the vegetables are softened.

3 Stir in the tomato and chick-peas, then add the couscous. Adjust the seasoning and stir over medium heat, until hot. Serve garnished with fresh cilantro sprigs.

Spicy Chicken and Rice

This dish is a complete meal on its own, but is also delicious served with a lentil dish such as Tarka Dhal.

Serves 4

INGREDIENTS
2 cups basmati rice
2 tablespoons olive oil
1 onion, sliced
¼ teaspoon mixed onion and
  mustard seeds
3 curry leaves
1 teaspoon grated fresh ginger
1 clove garlic, crushed
1 teaspoon ground coriander
1 teaspoon chili powder
1½ teaspoons salt
2 tomatoes, sliced
1 potato, cubed
½ cup frozen peas
6 ounces boned and skinned
  chicken breast, cubed
4 tablespoons chopped fresh
  cilantro
2 fresh green chilies, chopped
3 cups water

1 Rinse the rice in several changes of cold water, then soak in fresh cold water for 30 minutes. Drain and set aside. In a non-stick saucepan, heat the oil and fry the sliced onion until golden.

2 Add the onion and mustard seeds, the curry leaves, ginger, garlic, ground coriander, chili powder and salt. Stir-fry for about 2 minutes.

3 Add the sliced tomatoes, cubed potato, thawed peas and cubed chicken and mix well.

4 Add the rice and stir gently to combine with the other ingredients.

chicken

olive oil

onion

ground coriander

chili powder

mustard seeds

curry leaves

tomatoes

green chilies

ginger

potato

garlic

fresh cilantro

frozen peas

basmati rice

5 Finally, add the fresh cilantro and chopped green chilies. Mix well. Toss over the heat for 1 more minute. Pour in the water. Bring to a boil and reduce the heat to the lowest setting. Cover and cook for about 20 minutes, by which time all the liquid should have been absorbed and the mixture should be fragrant. Serve immediately.

NUTRITIONAL NOTES

PER PORTION:

CALORIES 406
FAT 8.5 g **SATURATED FAT** 1.9 g
CHOLESTEROL 25.1 mg

Chicken Kebabs and Rice

This marinade contains sugar and will burn very easily, so grill the kebabs slowly, turning often. Serve with Harlequin Rice.

Serves 4

INGREDIENTS
2 boned and skinned chicken breasts
8 pickling onions or 2 medium
  onions, peeled
4 lean bacon rashers
3 firm bananas
1 red pepper, seeded and diced

FOR THE MARINADE
2 tbsp brown sugar
1 tbsp Worcestershire sauce
2 tbsp lemon juice
salt and freshly ground black pepper

FOR THE HARLEQUIN RICE
2 tbsp olive oil
generous 1 cup cooked rice
1 cup cooked peas
1 small red pepper, seeded and diced

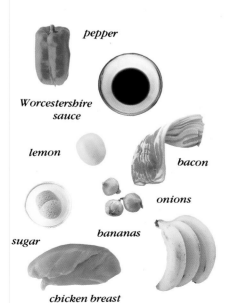

pepper

Worcestershire sauce

lemon

bacon

onions

sugar

bananas

chicken breast

1 Mix together the marinade ingredients. Cut each chicken breast into four pieces, add to the marinade, cover and leave for at least four hours or preferably overnight.

2 Peel the pickling onions, blanch them in boiling water for 5 minutes and drain. If using medium onions, quarter them after blanching.

3 Cut each rasher of bacon in half. Peel the bananas and cut each into three pieces. Wrap a rasher of bacon around each piece of banana.

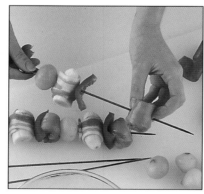

4 Thread onto metal skewers with the chicken pieces, onions and pepper pieces. Brush with the marinade.

5 Broil or barbecue over low coals for 15 minutes, turning and basting frequently with the marinade. Keep warm while you prepare the rice.

70

COOK'S TIP

Pour boiling water over the small onions and then drain, to make peeling easier.

NUTRITIONAL NOTES

Per portion:

CALORIES 419
FAT 14.1 g **SATURATED FAT** 4.6 g
CHOLESTEROL 51.7 mg

6 Heat the oil in a frying pan and add the rice, peas and diced pepper. Stir the mixture until heated through and serve with the kebabs.

Chicken and Rice Stir-fry

This dish is originally from Thailand, but can easily be adapted by adding any cooked ingredients you have to hand. Crispy shrimp crackers make an ideal accompaniment.

Serves 4

INGREDIENTS
8 oz long grain rice
2 large eggs
2 tbsp vegetable oil
1 green chili
2 scallions, roughly chopped
2 cloves garlic, crushed
8 oz cooked chicken
8 oz cooked shrimp
3 tbsp dark soy sauce
shrimp crackers, to serve

rice

soy sauce

egg

chili

shrimp

NUTRITIONAL NOTES

PER PORTION:

CALORIES 423
FAT 10.4 g **SATURATED FAT** 2.3 g
CHOLESTEROL 184.6 mg

1 Rinse the rice and then cook for 10–12 minutes in 2 cups water in a saucepan with a tight-fitting lid. When cooked, refresh under cold water.

2 Lightly beat the eggs. Heat 1 tbsp of oil in a small frying pan and swirl in the beaten egg. When cooked on one side, flip over and cook on the other side, remove from the pan and leave to cool. Cut the omelet into strips.

3 Carefully remove the seeds from the chili and chop finely, wearing rubber gloves to protect your hands if necessary. Place the scallions, chili and garlic in a food processor and blend to a paste.

4 Heat the wok, and then add the remaining oil. When the oil is hot, add the paste and stir-fry for 1 minute.

5 Add the chicken and shrimp.

6 Add the rice and stir-fry for 3–4 minutes. Stir in the soy sauce and serve with shrimp crackers.

Caribbean Chicken Kebabs

These kebabs have a rich, robust flavor and the marinade keeps them moist without the need for oil. Serve with a colorful salad and rice.

Serves 4

INGREDIENTS

1¼ pounds boned and skinned chicken breasts
finely grated rind of 1 lime
2 tablespoons fresh lime juice
1 tablespoon rum or sherry
1 tablespoon light brown sugar
1 teaspoon ground cinnamon
2 mangoes, peeled and cubed

chicken

lime

rum

light brown sugar

ground cinnamon

mango

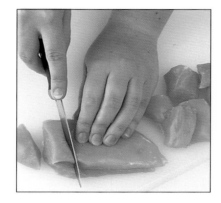

1 Cut the chicken into bite-size chunks and place in a bowl with the lime rind and juice, rum or sherry, sugar and cinnamon. Toss well, cover and let stand for 1 hour.

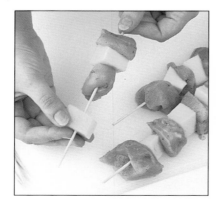

2 Drain the chicken, saving the juices and thread onto four wooden skewers, alternating with the mango cubes.

3 Broil the skewers or cook on a hot barbecue for 8–10 minutes, turning occasionally and basting with the juices, until the chicken is tender and golden brown. Serve with rice and salad.

COOK'S TIP

Soak the skewers in cold water for 30 minutes before filling them. This prevents the wood from scorching.

NUTRITIONAL NOTES

PER PORTION:

CALORIES 218
FAT 4.2 g **SATURATED FAT** 1.3 g
CHOLESTEROL 53.8 mg

Chicken Fried Noodles

This delicious dish makes a filling meal. Take care when frying vermicelli as it has a tendency to spit when added to hot oil.

Serves 4

INGREDIENTS
½ cup vegetable oil
8 oz rice vermicelli
5 oz green beans, topped, tailed and halved lengthwise
1 onion, finely chopped
2 boneless, skinless chicken breasts, about 6 oz each, cut into strips
1 tsp chili powder
8 oz cooked shrimp
3 tbsp dark soy sauce
3 tbsp white wine vinegar
2 tsp superfine sugar
fresh coriander sprigs, to garnish

rice vermicelli

chicken breast

onion

green beans

shrimp

NUTRITIONAL NOTES
PER PORTION:

CALORIES 487
FAT 15 g **SATURATED FAT** 2.6 g
CHOLESTEROL 83.2 mg

1 Heat the wok, then add 4 tbsp of the oil. Break up the vermicelli into 3 in lengths. When the oil is hot, fry the vermicelli in batches. Remove from the heat and keep warm.

2 Heat the remaining oil in the wok, then add the green beans, onion and chicken and stir-fry for 3 minutes until the chicken is cooked.

3 Sprinkle in the chili powder. Stir in the shrimp, soy sauce, vinegar and sugar, and stir-fry for 2 minutes.

4 Serve the chicken, shrimp and vegetables on the vermicelli, garnished with sprigs of fresh coriander.

Tortellini

Serves 6–8 as a starter or 4–6 as a main course

INGREDIENTS
4 ounces smoked lean ham
4 ounces chicken breast, boned and
  skinned
3¾ cups chicken or vegetable stock
cilantro stalks
2 tablespoons grated Parmesan
  cheese, plus extra for serving
1 egg, beaten, plus egg white
  for brushing
2 tablespoons chopped
  fresh cilantro
1 recipe basic pasta dough
flour, for dusting
salt and ground black pepper
cilantro leaves, to garnish

basic pasta
dough

smoked
ham

chicken
breast

grated Parmesan
cheese

stock

cilantro

egg

1 Cut the ham and chicken into large chunks and put them into a saucepan with ⅔ cup of the chicken or vegetable stock and some cilantro stalks. Bring to a boil, cover and simmer for 20 minutes until tender. Cool the stock slightly.

2 Drain the ham and chicken and mince finely (reserve the stock). Put into a bowl with the Parmesan cheese, beaten egg, chopped cilantro and season with salt and pepper.

3 Roll the pasta into thin sheets, cut into 1½-inch squares. Put ½ teaspoon of filling on each. Brush edges with egg white and fold each square into a triangle; press out any air and seal firmly.

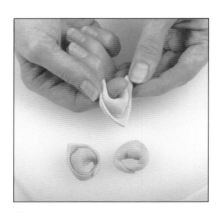

4 Curl each triangle around the tip of a forefinger and press the two ends together firmly.

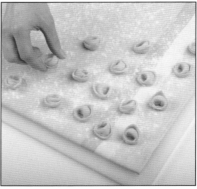

5 Lay on a lightly floured tea towel to rest for 30 minutes before cooking.

NUTRITIONAL NOTES
PER PORTION:

CALORIES 335
FAT 9.7 g **SATURATED FAT** 3.6 g
CHOLESTEROL 193 mg

6 Strain the reserved stock and add to the remainder. Put into a pan and bring to a boil. Lower the heat to a gentle boil and add the tortellini. Cook for 5 minutes. Then turn off the heat, cover the pan and let stand for 20–30 minutes. Serve in soup plates with some of the stock and garnish with cilantro leaves. Serve grated Parmesan separately.

Chicken Kiev

Cut through the crispy-coated chicken to reveal a creamy filling with just a hint of garlic.

Serves 4

INGREDIENTS
4 large chicken breasts, boned and
    skinned
1 tbsp lemon juice
½ cup ricotta cheese
1 garlic clove, crushed
2 tbsp chopped fresh parsley
¼ tsp freshly grated nutmeg
2 tbsp flour
pinch of cayenne pepper
¼ tsp salt
2 cups fresh white bread
    crumbs
2 egg whites, lightly beaten
duchesse potatoes, green beans and
    broiled tomatoes, to serve

bread crumbs

egg whites

chicken breast

ricotta cheese

garlic

parsley

1 Preheat the oven to 400°F. Place the chicken breasts between two sheets of plastic wrap and gently beat with a rolling pin until flattened. Sprinkle with the lemon juice.

2 Mix the ricotta cheese with the garlic, 1 tbsp of the chopped parsley, and the nutmeg. Shape into four 2-in long cylinders.

3 Put one portion of the cheese and herb mixture in the center of each chicken breast and fold the meat over, tucking in the edges to enclose the filling completely.

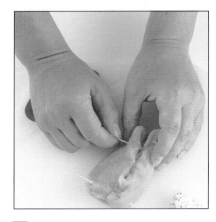

4 Secure the chicken with toothpicks pushed through the center of each. Mix together the flour, cayenne pepper and salt. Dust the chicken with the flour.

5 Mix together the bread crumbs and remaining parsley. Dip the chicken into the egg whites, then coat with the bread crumbs. Chill for 30 minutes in the refrigerator, then dip into the egg white and bread crumbs for a second time.

NUTRITIONAL NOTES
PER PORTION:

CALORIES 354.5
FAT 9.0 g **SATURATED FAT** 3.5 g
CHOLESTEROL 78.9 mg

6 Put the chicken on a non-stick baking sheet and spray with non-stick cooking spray. Bake in the preheated oven for 25 minutes or until the coating is golden brown and the chicken completely cooked. Remove the toothpicks and serve with duchesse potatoes, green beans and broiled tomatoes.

Minty Yogurt Chicken

Honey, lime juice and fresh mint make a
marvelous marinade.

Serves 4

INGREDIENTS
8 skinned chicken thigh portions
1 tablespoon clear honey
2 tablespoons lime juice
2 tablespoons low fat plain yogurt
¼ cup chopped fresh mint
salt and ground black pepper

chicken thighs

honey

lime juice

plain yogurt

mint

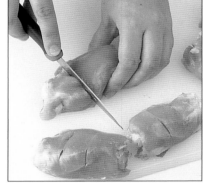

I Slash the chicken at intervals with a
sharp knife. Place in a bowl.

2 Mix the honey, lime juice, yogurt and
half the mint in a bowl. Add salt and
pepper to taste.

3 Spoon the marinade over the
chicken. Cover and set aside for
30 minutes.

4 Line a broiler pan with foil and cook
the chicken under a moderately hot
broiler until thoroughly cooked and
golden brown, turning the portions
occasionally during cooking. Sprinkle with
remaining mint, and serve. Potatoes and
a tomato salad are all you need as
accompaniments.

NUTRITIONAL NOTES
PER PORTION:

CALORIES 171
FAT 6.7 g **SATURATED FAT** 2.2 g
CHOLESTEROL 97.9 mg

Chicken in Creamy Orange Sauce

This sauce is deceptively creamy – in fact it is made with low fat cream cheese, which is virtually fat-free. The brandy adds a richer flavor, but is optional – omit it if you prefer and use orange juice on its own.

Serves 4

INGREDIENTS
8 skinned chicken thighs or
   drumsticks
3 tablespoons brandy
1¼ cups orange juice
3 scallions, chopped
2 teaspoons cornstarch
6 tablespoons low fat cream cheese
salt and ground black pepper

chicken thighs

brandy

scallions

cornstarch

cream cheese

1 Fry the chicken pieces without fat in a non-stick frying pan, turning until evenly browned.

2 Stir in the brandy, orange juice and scallions. Bring to a boil, then cover and simmer for 15 minutes or until the chicken is tender and the juices run clear, not pink, when pierced.

3 Blend the cornstarch with a little water then stir into the cream cheese. Stir into the sauce and stir over medium heat until thickened.

4 Adjust the seasoning and serve with boiled rice or pasta and green salad.

NUTRITIONAL NOTES
PER PORTION:

CALORIES 227
FAT 6.8 g **SATURATED FAT** 2.2 g
CHOLESTEROL 87.8 mg

Chicken and Pineapple Kebabs

This chicken has a delicate tang and is very tender. The pineapple gives a slight sweetness to the chicken.

Serves 6

INGREDIENTS
8-ounce can pineapple chunks in natural juice
1 teaspoon ground cumin
1 teaspoon ground coriander
1 small garlic clove, crushed
1 teaspoon chili powder
1 teaspoon salt
2 tablespoons low-fat plain yogurt
1 tablespoon chopped fresh cilantro
few drops of orange food coloring (optional)
10 ounces skinned and boned chicken breasts
½ red bell pepper
½ yellow or green bell pepper
1 large onion
6 cherry tomatoes
2 teaspoons corn oil

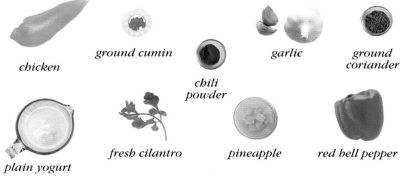

chicken

ground cumin

garlic

ground coriander

chili powder

plain yogurt

fresh cilantro

pineapple

red bell pepper

yellow bell pepper

onion

cherry tomatoes

corn oil

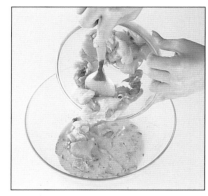

 Drain the pineapple juice into a bowl. Reserve twelve large chunks of pineapple and squeeze the juice from the remaining chunks into the bowl and set aside. You should have about ½ cup of pineapple juice. Make up with water if necessary.

 In a large mixing bowl, combine the ground cumin, ground coriander, garlic, chili powder, salt, yogurt, fresh cilantro and food coloring, if using. Pour in the reserved pineapple juice and mix well.

 Cut the chicken into bite-size cubes, add to the yogurt and spice mixture, cover and let marinate for 1–1½ hours. Meanwhile cut the peppers and onion into bite-size chunks.

 Preheat the broiler to medium. Drain the chicken pieces, reserving the marinade, and thread on to six wooden or metal skewers, alternating with the vegetables and reserved pineapple chunks.

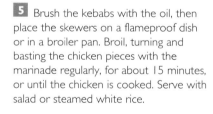 Brush the kebabs with the oil, then place the skewers on a flameproof dish or in a broiler pan. Broil, turning and basting the chicken pieces with the marinade regularly, for about 15 minutes, or until the chicken is cooked. Serve with salad or steamed white rice.

NUTRITIONAL NOTES
PER PORTION:

CALORIES 170
FAT 6.7 g **SATURATED FAT** 1.5 g
CHOLESTEROL 40.6 mg

Chicken with Orange and Mustard Sauce

The beauty of this recipe is its simplicity; the chicken continues to cook in its own juices while you prepare the sauce.

Serves 4

INGREDIENTS
2 large oranges
4 chicken breasts, boned and skinned
1 tsp sunflower oil
salt and freshly ground black pepper
baby potatoes and sliced zucchini
   tossed in parsley, to serve

FOR THE ORANGE AND MUSTARD SAUCE
2 tsp cornstarch
⅔ cup strained yogurt
1 tsp Dijon mustard

chicken breast

yogurt

cornstarch

mustard

orange

NUTRITIONAL NOTES
PER PORTION:

CALORIES 215
FAT 5.4 g **SATURATED FAT** 1.7 g
CHOLESTEROL 55.3 mg

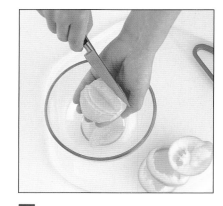

1 Peel the oranges using a sharp knife, removing all the white pith. Remove the segments by cutting between the membranes, holding the fruit over a small bowl to catch any juice. Set aside with the juice until required.

2 Season the chicken with salt and freshly ground black pepper. Heat the oil in a non-stick frying pan and cook the chicken for 5 minutes on each side. Take out of the frying pan and wrap in foil; the meat will continue to cook for a while.

3 For the sauce, blend together the cornstarch with the juice from the orange. Add the yogurt and mustard. Put into the frying pan and slowly bring to a boil. Simmer for 1 minute.

4 Add the orange segments to the sauce and heat gently. Unwrap the chicken and add any excess juices to the sauce. Slice on the diagonal and serve with the sauce, baby potatoes and sliced zucchini tossed in parsley.

Moroccan Spiced Roast Poussins

This combination of dried fruit and spices is typical of North African cooking.

Serves 4

INGREDIENTS

1 cup cooked long grain rice, plus
  extra for serving
1 small onion, finely chopped
finely grated rind and juice of
  1 lemon
2 tablespoons chopped fresh mint
3 tablespoons chopped
  dried apricots
2 tablespoons low fat
  plain yogurt
2 teaspoons ground turmeric
2 teaspoons ground cumin
2 poussins, each about 1 pound
salt and ground black pepper
lemon slices and fresh mint sprigs,

long grain rice   *onion*

lemon

dried apricots

mint

ground cumin

ground turmeric

poussins   *plain yogurt*

1 Preheat the oven to 400°F. Mix the rice, onion, lemon rind, mint and apricots in a bowl. Stir in half each of the lemon juice, yogurt, turmeric and cumin. Season with salt and pepper.

2 Stuff the neck of the birds with the rice. Place the birds on a rack in a roasting pan.

NUTRITIONAL NOTES

PER PORTION:

CALORIES 219
FAT 6.0 g **SATURATED FAT** 1.9 g
CHOLESTEROL 71.6 mg

3 Combine the remaining lemon juice, yogurt, turmeric and cumin, then brush this over the poussins. Cover loosely with foil and roast for 30 minutes.

4 Remove the foil and roast for another 15 minutes or until the birds are golden brown and the juices run clear, not pink, when pierced.

5 Cut the birds in half with a sharp knife or poultry shears, and serve with cooked rice, if you wish. Garnish with lemon and fresh mint.

Chicken with Green Mango

Green, unripe mango is used for making various Indian dishes, including this simple chicken dish.

NUTRITIONAL NOTES
Per portion:
CALORIES 269
FAT 11.0 g SATURATED FAT 2.4 g
CHOLESTEROL 64.1 mg

Serves 4

INGREDIENTS
1 medium green (unripe) mango
1 pound boned and skinned
  chicken breasts, cubed
¼ teaspoon onion seeds
1 teaspoon grated fresh ginger
1 small garlic clove, crushed
1 teaspoon chili powder
¼ teaspoon ground turmeric
1 teaspoon salt
1 teaspoon ground coriander
2 tablespoons corn oil
2 onions, sliced
4 curry leaves
1¼ cups water
2 tomatoes, quartered
2 fresh green chilies, chopped
2 tablespoons fresh cilantro

1 Peel the mango and slice the flesh thickly. Discard the pit. Place the mango slices in a bowl, cover and set aside.

2 Place the chicken cubes in a bowl and add the onion seeds, ginger, garlic, chili powder, turmeric, salt and ground coriander. Mix the spices into the chicken and add half the mango slices to this mixture as well.

3 In a medium saucepan, heat the oil and fry the sliced onions until golden brown. Add the curry leaves.

chicken

turmeric

ginger

onion seeds

garlic

chili powder

green mango

corn oil

fresh cilantro

onion

ground coriander

curry leaves

tomatoes

green chilies

4 Gradually add the spiced chicken cubes, stirring all the time.

5 Pour in the water, bring to a boil, then lower the heat and cook for 12–15 minutes, stirring occasionally, until the chicken is cooked through and the water has evaporated.

6 Add the remaining mango slices, the tomatoes, green chilies and fresh cilantro. Mix lightly and serve.

Chicken Roll

The roll can be prepared and cooked the day before and will freeze well too. Remove from the refrigerator about an hour before serving.

Serves 8

INGREDIENTS
1 × 4 lb chicken

FOR THE STUFFING
1 medium onion, finely chopped
4 tbsp melted butter
12 oz lean ground pork
4 rashers lean bacon, chopped
1 tbsp chopped fresh parsley
2 tsp chopped fresh thyme
2 cups fresh white bread crumbs
2 tbsp sherry
1 large egg, beaten
¼ cup shelled unsalted pistachio nuts
¼ cup pitted black olives (about 12)
salt and freshly ground black pepper

1 To make the stuffing, cook the chopped onion gently in 2 tbsp of the butter until soft. Turn into a bowl and cool. Add the remaining ingredients, mix thoroughly and season with salt and freshly ground black pepper.

2 To bone the chicken, use a small, sharp knife to remove the wing tips (pinions). Turn the chicken onto its breast and cut a line down the back bone.

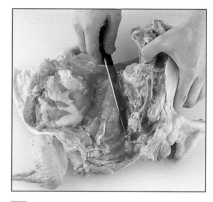

3 Cut the flesh away from the carcass, scraping the bones clean. Carefully cut through the sinew around the leg and wing joints and scrape down the bones to free them. Remove the carcass, taking care not to cut through the skin along the breast bone.

black olives

bread crumbs

thyme

onion

pork

butter

bacon

4 To stuff the chicken, lay it flat, skin side down and level the flesh as much as possible. Shape the stuffing down the center of the chicken and fold the sides over the stuffing.

5 Sew the flesh neatly together, using a needle and dark thread. Tie with fine string into a roll.

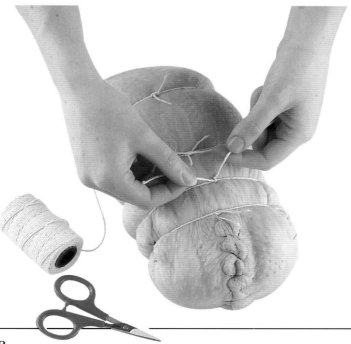

COOK'S TIPS

Thaw the chicken roll from frozen for 12 hours in the refrigerator, and leave to stand at cool room temperature for an hour before serving.

Use dark thread for sewing, as it is much easier to see so that you can remove it once the roll is cooked.

NUTRITIONAL NOTES

Per portion:

CALORIES 235
FAT 14.9 g **SATURATED FAT** 4.4 g
CHOLESTEROL 99.7 mg

6 Preheat the oven to 350°F. Place the roll, with the join underneath, on a roasting rack in a roasting pan and brush generously with the remaining butter. Bake uncovered for about 1 ¼ hours or until cooked. Baste the chicken often with the juices in the roasting pan. Leave to cool completely before removing the string and thread. Wrap in foil and chill until ready for serving or freezing.

Chili Chicken

Serve as a simple supper dish with boiled potatoes and broccoli, or as a party dish with rice.

Serves 4

INGREDIENTS
12 chicken thighs
1 tbsp olive oil
1 medium onion, thinly sliced
1 garlic clove, crushed
1 tsp chili powder or 1 fresh chili, chopped
1 × 14 oz can chopped tomatoes, with their juice
1 tsp superfine sugar
1 × 15 oz can red kidney beans, drained
salt and freshly ground black pepper

red kidney beans

tomatoes

onion

olive oil

garlic

chicken thighs

superfine sugar

chili powder

1 Cut the chicken into large cubes, removing all skin and bones. Heat the oil in a large flameproof casserole and brown the chicken pieces on all sides. Remove and keep warm.

2 Add the onion and garlic clove to the casserole and cook until tender. Add the chili powder or fresh chili and cook for 2 minutes. Add the tomatoes with their juice, seasoning and sugar.

NUTRITIONAL NOTES
PER PORTION:

CALORIES 352
FAT 13.4 g **SATURATED FAT** 3.8 g
CHOLESTEROL 131.4 mg

3 Replace the chicken pieces, cover the casserole and simmer for about 30 minutes until tender.

4 Add the red kidney beans and gently cook for a further 5 minutes to heat them through before serving.

Citrus Kebabs

Serve on a bed of lettuce leaves and garnish with fresh mint and orange and lemon slices.

Serves 4

INGREDIENTS
4 chicken breasts, skinned and boned
fresh mint sprigs, to garnish
orange, lemon or lime slices, to
    garnish (optional)

FOR THE MARINADE
finely grated rind and juice of
    ½ orange
finely grated rind and juice of ½ small
    lemon or lime
2 tbsp olive oil
2 tbsp honey
2 tbsp chopped fresh mint
¼ tsp ground cumin
salt and freshly ground black pepper

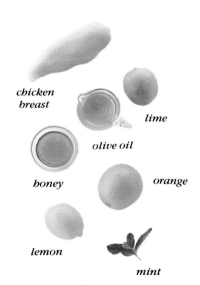

chicken breast

lime

olive oil

honey

orange

lemon

mint

NUTRITIONAL NOTES
PER PORTION:

CALORIES 229
FAT 9.6 g **SATURATED FAT** 2.1 g
CHOLESTEROL 53.8 mg

1 Cut the chicken into cubes of approximately 1 in.

2 Mix the marinade ingredients together, add the chicken cubes and leave to marinade for at least 2 hours.

3 Thread the chicken pieces onto skewers and broil or barbecue over low coals for 15 minutes, basting with the marinade and turning frequently. Serve garnished with extra mint and citrus slices if desired.

Tagine of Chicken

Based on a traditional Moroccan dish. The chicken and couscous can be cooked the day before and reheated for serving.

Serves 8

INGREDIENTS
8 chicken legs (thighs and
    drumsticks)
2 tbsp olive oil
1 medium onion, finely chopped
2 garlic cloves, crushed
1 tsp ground turmeric
½ tsp ground ginger
½ tsp ground cinnamon
scant 2 cups fresh or canned chicken
    stock
1¼ cups pitted green olives
1 lemon, sliced
salt and freshly ground black pepper
fresh coriander sprigs, to garnish

FOR THE VEGETABLE COUSCOUS
2½ cups fresh or canned chicken
    stock
1 lb couscous
4 zucchini, thickly sliced
2 carrots, thickly sliced
2 small turnips, peeled and cubed
3 tbsp olive oil
1 × 15 oz can chick peas, drained

cinnamon
ginger
turmeric
green olives
onion
couscous
lemon
turnip
garlic
coriander
carrot
chick peas
zucchini
chicken stock
olive oil
chicken

1 Preheat the oven to 350°F. Cut the chicken legs into two through the joint.

2 Heat the oil in a large flameproof casserole and working in batches, brown the chicken on both sides. Remove and keep warm.

3 Add the onion and crushed garlic to the flameproof casserole and cook gently until tender. Add the spices and cook for 1 minute. Pour over the stock, bring to a boil, and return the chicken. Cover and bake for 45 minutes until tender.

4 Transfer the chicken to a bowl, cover and keep warm. Remove any fat from the cooking liquid and boil to reduce by one-third. Meanwhile, blanch the olives and lemon slices in a pan of boiling water for 2 minutes until the lemon skin is tender. Drain and add to the cooking liquid, adjusting the seasoning to taste.

5 To cook the couscous, bring the stock to a boil in a large pan and sprinkle in the couscous slowly, stirring all the time. Remove from the heat, cover and leave to stand for 5 minutes.

COOK'S TIP

The couscous can be reheated with 2 tbsp olive oil in a steamer over a pan of boiling water, stirring occasionally. If you cook the chicken in advance, undercook it by 15 minutes and reheat in the oven for 20–30 minutes.

NUTRITIONAL NOTES

PER PORTION:

CALORIES 350
FAT 10.8 g **SATURATED FAT** 2.3 g
CHOLESTEROL 65.7 mg

6 Meanwhile, cook the vegetables, drain and put them into a large bowl. Add the couscous and oil and season. Stir the grains to fluff them up, add the chick peas and finally the chopped coriander. Spoon onto a large serving plate, cover with the chicken pieces, and spoon over the liquid. Garnish with fresh coriander sprigs.

Chicken with Shrimp

For this extra-special party dish, the skin is left on the chicken for extra flavor, but the general fat content is reduced by low fat cooking techniques.

Serves 4

INGREDIENTS
1 chicken (3–3½ pounds), cut
  into 8 pieces
2 teaspoons corn oil
12 large raw shrimp
1 small onion, halved and sliced
2 tablespoons flour
¾ cup dry white wine
2 tablespoons brandy
1¼ cups defatted
  chicken broth
3 tomatoes, cored and quartered
1 or 2 garlic cloves, finely chopped
bouquet garni
¼ cup reduced-fat
  whipping cream
salt and ground black pepper
fresh parsley, to garnish

COOK'S TIP

To prepare ahead, cook as directed up to step 5. Cool and chill the chicken and sauce. To serve, reheat the chicken and sauce over medium-low heat for about 30 minutes. Add the shrimp tails and heat through.

1 Wash the chicken pieces, then pat dry with kitchen paper and season with salt and pepper. Heat the oil in a flame-proof casserole and cook the shrimp over high heat until they turn a bright color. Remove the shrimp, cool slightly and then peel away the heads and shells and reserve. Chill the peeled tails.

2 Add the chicken to the casserole, skin side down, and cook over medium-high heat for 10–12 minutes until golden brown, turning to color evenly and cooking in batches if necessary. Transfer the chicken to a plate and pour off all but 1 tablespoon of the fat.

3 In the same casserole, cook the onion over medium-high heat until golden, stirring frequently. Sprinkle with flour and continue cooking for 2 minutes, stirring frequently, then add the wine and brandy and bring to a boil, stirring constantly.

chicken

corn oil

flour

garlic

large shrimp

white wine

brandy

small onion

tomatoes

chicken broth

bouquet garni

whipping cream

NUTRITIONAL NOTES
PER PORTION:

CALORIES 446
FAT 13.0 g **SATURATED FAT** 4.4 g
CHOLESTEROL 292 mg

4 Add the broth, shrimp heads and shells, tomatoes, garlic and bouquet garni with the chicken pieces and any juices. Bring to a boil, then cover the casserole and simmer for 20-25 minutes, or until the chicken is tender and the juices run clear when the thickest part of the meat is pierced.

5 Remove the chicken pieces from the casserole and strain the cooking liquid, pressing down on the shells and vegetables to extract as much liquid as possible. Skim off the fat from the cooking liquid and return the liquid to the pan. Add the cream and boil until it is reduced by one-third and slightly thickened.

6 Return the chicken pieces to the pan and simmer for 5 minutes. Just before serving, add the shrimp tails and heat through. Arrange on warmed plates, pour on some of the sauce and garnish with fresh parsley.